maran illustrated

Dog Training

maranGraphics™

&

THOMSON

COURSE TECHNOLOGY

Professional ■ Technical ■ Reference

MARAN ILLUSTRATED™ Dog Training

Distributed in the U.S. and Canada by Thomson Course Technology PTR. For enquiries about Maran Illustrated™ books outside the U.S. and Canada, please contact maranGraphics at international@maran.com

For U.S. orders and customer service, please contact Thomson Course Technology at 1-800-354-9706. For Canadian orders, please contact Thomson Course Technology at 1-800-268-2222 or 416-752-9448.

ISBN-13: 978-1-59200-858-2
ISBN-10: 1-59200-858-5

Library of Congress Catalog Card Number: 2005921011

Printed in the United States of America

05 06 07 08 09 BU 10 9 8 7

Trademarks

Important

maranGraphics and Thomson Course Technology PTR cannot provide software support. Please contact the appropriate software manufacturer's technical support line or Web site for assistance.

maranGraphics and Thomson Course Technology PTR have attempted throughout this book to distinguish proprietary trademarks by following the capitalization style used by the source. However, we cannot attest to the accuracy of the style, and the use of a word or term in this book is not intended to affect the validity of any trademark.

Copies

Educational facilities, companies, and organizations located in the U.S. and Canada that are interested in multiple copies of this book should contact Thomson Course Technology PTR for quantity discount information. Training manuals, CD-ROMs, and portions of this book are also available individually or can be tailored for specific needs.

maranGraphics™

maranGraphics Inc.
5755 Coopers Avenue
Mississauga, Ontario
L4Z 1R9
www.maran.com

THOMSON
COURSE TECHNOLOGY
Professional ■ Technical ■ Reference

Thomson Course Technology PTR, a division of Thomson Course Technology
25 Thomson Place ■ Boston, MA 02210 ■ http://www.courseptr.com

maranGraphics is a family-run business

At **maranGraphics**, we believe in producing great consumer books–one book at a time.

Each maranGraphics book uses the award-winning communication process that we have been developing over the last 30 years. Using this process, we organize photographs and text in a way that makes it easy for you to learn new concepts and tasks.

We spend hours deciding the best way to perform each task, so you don't have to! Our clear, easy-to-follow photographs and instructions walk you through each task from beginning to end.

We want to thank you for purchasing what we feel are the best books money can buy. We hope you enjoy using this book as much as we enjoyed creating it!

Sincerely,

The Maran Family

We would love to hear from you! Send your comments and feedback about our books to family@maran.com

Please visit us on the Web at:
www.maran.com

CREDITS

Author:
maranGraphics Development Group

Content Architects:
Kelleigh Johnson
Wanda Lawrie

Technical Consultant:
Lisa Roussac Kruitwagen BA, CPDT

Project Manager:
Judy Maran

Copy Development Director:
Jill Maran Dutfield

Copy Developers:
Michael B. Kelly
Cathy Lo
Adam Giles
Raquel Scott

Editor:
Adam Giles

Layout Designer:
Richard Hung

**Front Cover Image and
Overview Designer:**
Russ Marini

Photographic Retouching:
Russ Marini
Richard Hung

Dog Model Coordinator:
Lorraine Houston

Indexer:
Kelleigh Johnson

Photography and Post Production:
Robert Maran

**President,
Thomson Course Technology:**
David R. West

**Senior Vice President of
Business Development,
Thomson Course Technology:**
Andy Shafran

**Publisher and General Manager,
Thomson Course Technology PTR:**
Stacy L. Hiquet

**Associate Director
of Marketing,
Thomson Course Technology PTR:**
Sarah O'Donnell

**National Sales Manager,
Thomson Course Technology PTR:**
Amy Merrill

**Manager of Editorial Services,
Thomson Course Technology PTR:**
Heather Talbot

ACKNOWLEDGMENTS

Thanks to the dedicated staff of maranGraphics, including Adam Giles,
Richard Hung, Kelleigh Johnson, Wanda Lawrie, Jill Maran Dutfield,
Judy Maran, Robert Maran, Ruth Maran, Russ Marini and Raquel Scott.

Finally, to Richard Maran who originated the easy-to-use graphic format
of this guide. Thank you for your inspiration and guidance.

Lisa Roussac Kruitwagen BA, CPDT

Lisa Roussac Kruitwagen has combined a deep love for dogs with a commitment to help families enjoy pet guardianship. As the owner of Dealing with Dogs Ltd., she and her committed staff offer puppy and dog obedience classes. Dealing with Dogs classes focus on building a lasting relationship with our canine companions through positive training methods. Lisa is a member of the American Association of Pet Dog Trainers, The Canadian Association of Pet Dog Trainers and the Canadian Kennel Club.

She is also independently certified by the Certification Council for Pet Dog Trainers through the Professional Testing Corporation of New York. Lisa has made local television appearances as a guest expert and has contributed articles to City Dog magazine. Lisa also competes in numerous dog-related activities with her own dogs and has a keen interest in horses. Lisa and her husband share their life with four children, three dogs and a sweet Morgan mare.

About the Dog Model Coordinator...

Lorraine Houston

Since 1976, Lorraine Houston has been involved with the plight of homeless, abandoned dogs and has worked in shelters in the U.S. and Canada.

Lorraine is the author of *Nobody's Best Friend* and in 2003 won the Dog Writers Association of America Maxwell Award for her story "Barry." She is also a writer for the *Mirror* and *Dogs, Dogs, Dogs!* newspapers.

In addition, Lorraine is an evaluator for Therapeutic Paws of Canada and St. John Ambulance Therapy Dogs. She is also a member of the Canadian Association of Professional Pet Dog Trainers and the director of Speaking of Dogs.

Lorraine is an advocate for humane training, rescue/shelter dog adoptions and relationships built on kindness and respect. She has fostered over 300 dogs and found homes for thousands more.

Special thanks to...

- Naomi Kane for supplying Leonberger puppies. Leonberger puppies bred by Naomi Kane, Lewenhart Registered.
- Dogeden for allowing us to show photographs of their dog daycare. www.dogeden.com
- The American Kennel Club for allowing us to show their logo. www.akc.org
- Kong Company for allowing us to show photographs of their equipment. www.kongcompany.com

Thank you to the following dogs and owners for participating in the photos for the "Guide to Popular Dog Breeds" topic.

Labrador Retriever: Phantom (Victoria Vidal-Ribas)
Golden Retriever: Cody (Brenda Meloche)
American Cocker Spaniel: Smithwicks (Trudy Cochrane)
German Shorthaired Pointer: Sam (Connie Cohen)
Yorkshire Terrier: Timmy (Gayle Skrien)
Shih Tzu: Cookie (Geoffrey & Gail Ralph)
Chihuahua: Elmo (Lillianne Ranaki)
Pug: Puggy Sue (Joan Weston)
Miniature Schnauzer: Benz (Patricia Pierpoint)
West Highland White Terrier: Jordan (Kathleen Barry)
Scottish Terrier: Max (Elayna Gualtieri)
Airedale Terrier: Tessa (Wendy Burton)
Beagle: Lynden (Cliff Tomas)
Dachshund: Jersey (Stacey Lewis)

Basset Hound: Daisy (Gertie Terry)
Greyhound: Max (Peter Molnar)
Boxer: Lexi (Tammy Johnston)
Rottweiler: Donnie (Dianna Contin)
Doberman Pinscher: Mandi (Enid Curd)
Siberian Husky: Niko (Ellie Luciani)
German Shepherd: Coco (Kade & Jill Dutfield)
Shetland Sheepdog: Emma (Kelly Doherty)
Pembroke Welsh Corgi: Holly (Jennifer Allen)
Collie: Fadan (Cindy Trotman)
Poodle: Mr.Darcy (Melanie Kiss)
Bulldog: The Great Gazoo (Joan Weston)
Boston Terrier: Oakley (Cassandra Keefe)
Bichon Frise: Sally (Peggy Rosenzweig)

model credits

maranGraphics would like to thank all of our friends who participated in this book.

Albie
Shih Tzu
Stu Kellock &
Shelley Baker

Bandit
Border Collie Mix
Judith Dremin

Becky
*Cavalier King Charles
Spaniel*
Natasha Kruitwagen

Bill
Border Collie
Morgan Jarvis

Blitz
*Jack Russell Terrier/
Border Collie Mix*
Morgan Jarvis

Carnegie
Golden Retriever
Carrie Kruitwagen

Chevy
Great Dane
Debbie Reynolds

Chloe
Standard Poodle
Lyndon Hutchison-
Hounsell

Coco
German Shepherd
Kade and Jill
Dutfield

Crank
*Border Collie/
Australian Cattle Dog*
Sarah Mombourquette

Digby
Shih Tzu
Pam McNaughton

Fletch
Hound Mix
Karin Apfel

Griffyn
English Bulldog
Andrea Barker

Isla
Smooth Collie
Lisa Roussac
Kruitwagen

Joey
*Shetland Sheepdog/
Soft-Coated Wheaten*
Dawn Dorazio

Jordan
*West Highland
White Terrier*
Kathleen Barry

Kally
English Pointer Mix
Wendy Terry

Kara
Tibetan Terrier
Terri Jankelow

Lily
Shetland Sheepdog
Keiley Abbat

Mango
*Schnauzer/
Jack Russell Mix*
Keiley Abbat

Milo
Australian Shepherd
Heather and Rob Lies

Molly
Border Collie
Luan Egan

Munya
Australian Cattle Dog
Sarah Mombourquette

Nina
Chow Mix
Lorraine Houston

Oreo
Jack Russell Terrier Mix
Teresa Ridgway

Pebbles
*Nova Scotia Duck
Tolling Retriever*
Patrick McDermott

Pepper
Bluetick Coonhound
Phillip McGregor

Puggy Sue
Pug
Joan Weston

Radar
Labrador Retriever
Cathy & Colleen
Steacy

Riggs
*American Staffordshire
Terrier Mix*
Karyn and Dale Williams

Shana
*Cavalier King Charles
Spaniel*
Julie Byrd Clark

Smithwicks
*American
Cocker Spaniel*
Trudy Cochrane

Storm
Border Collie
Sarah Mombourquette

Suki
Golden Retriever
Selby Milner

Sunny
Labrador Retriever
Karin Apfel

Tassu
Vizsla
Mary-Lou Jenkins

Tess
*Soft-Coated
Wheaten Terrier*
Brenda Collinge

The Great Gazoo
Bulldog
Joan Weston

Tiger
Labrador Retriever
Cathy & Colleen
Steacy

Tucker
*Golden Retriever/
Standard Poodle Mix*
John & Jen Marchand

Winston
Golden Retriever
Rob Paterson

Zeus
Labrador Retriever
Garnet Siddall

Table of Contents

Table of Contents

considerations before getting a dog

Before you bring a dog into your home, there are several questions you should ask yourself to determine if a dog will fit into your life. For example: Can you make the time commitment dog ownership requires? Do you have the financial resources needed to care for a dog? Will your lifestyle accommodate a dog?

Owning a dog is a long-term commitment. It is important to remember that most dogs have a life span of 8 to 15 years. Before getting a dog, make sure you fully understand the time commitment required. When considering the financial commitment, you must take into account the cost of food, grooming and providing medical care for your new dog.

From feeding and exercising to spending quality time with him, your dog will demand regular attention from you. If you have children, a demanding work schedule or like to travel, you must think about whether your lifestyle can accommodate the demands of owning a dog.

Educating yourself about the responsibilities of dog ownership and carefully considering your life can help ensure you and your dog have a long and lasting relationship.

Do you have the time to care for a dog?

- A dog does not simply require an hour of your time per day for play and exercise. A dog is a 24-hour-a-day, 7-day-a-week commitment.

- Consider, also, that most dogs have a life span of 8 to 15 years. Having a dog is a long-term commitment.

Do you have the financial resources to care for a dog?

- The purchase price of a dog is minimal compared to the long-term cost of dog ownership.

- Consider the costs of food, grooming equipment, veterinary visits, leashes, toys, and all the other items your dog will need over the course of his entire life.

Is there a particularly good time of year to get a dog?

The best time to get a dog is when you can devote a great deal of individual and uninterrupted attention to your dog. During a vacation from work, for example, you and your new dog have the time to get to know one another. On the other hand, a holiday, such as Christmas or Thanksgiving, is not a good time to get a dog. Holidays are stressful enough without the additional demands of introducing a new dog to your home environment. If your new dog is a Christmas gift, try to delay the dog's actual arrival until after the holidays.

If you live in a region that experiences unpredictable winter weather, consider waiting until spring before getting a dog. The demands of late-night housetraining can be troublesome in the snow and bitter cold.

Can your lifestyle accommodate a dog?

- The best time to get a dog is when children are over 6 years old.

- If you have other pets, consider how they will adjust to a new dog.

- If you travel frequently, remember that you will need to make arrangements to take your dog with you or have someone care for him while you are gone.

Where will the dog live?

- Dogs are social animals and are happiest when they live where they can socialize with their family. If you plan to have your dog live outside, you should reconsider getting a dog.

- Consider that some breeds need more space than others, due to their size or activity level. Some breeds also need a fenced yard to run in and are not suited to apartment life.

CONTINUED...

considerations before getting a dog (continued)

In addition to considering the time, money and lifestyle commitments dog ownership requires, you should assess whether you have the energy to exercise a dog and the patience to train and groom a dog.

Proper exercise and mental stimulation are essential to your dog's well being. Early and ongoing training helps your dog become a valued and loved member of your family and community. Regular grooming is an important aspect of keeping your dog clean and healthy. As a dog owner, you must accept responsibility for performing all of these duties. Even if your children promise to help you perform these tasks and take care of the dog, as the adult, the ultimate responsibility is yours.

The decision to bring a dog into your home is an important one. If you are prepared for and committed to dog ownership, your dog can be your best friend and constant companion. Keep in mind, however, that as a dog owner, you must be prepared to accept the very good with the occasionally inconvenient.

Would a puppy, adolescent or mature dog best suit you?

- Puppies under 6 months old require a lot of time, effort and patience.

- Adolescent dogs, between 6 and 18 months old, are full of energy and will test the boundaries of their environment.

- A mature dog may already be housetrained, socialized and trained in the basic commands.

Do you have the time and energy required to exercise a dog?

- Daily exercise is essential for all dogs. Be prepared to exercise your dog every day of his life.

- Consider whether you have the time, energy and desire to meet the physical needs of a dog.

- Different breeds of dogs have different activity levels. If you are not generally a physically active person, you may want to consider a dog with a low activity level.

Tip

How can I determine which breed of dog will best fit my lifestyle?

You can research each breed that you are interested in to find out which one will best fit your lifestyle. For example, living in a small home may dictate the purchase of a smaller breed of dog. Also, some breeds are easier to train than others, which is a consideration if you have limited time to devote to training. You can also attend dog shows, visit off-leash parks and take walks in popular dog walking areas to observe and meet different kinds of dogs and their owners.

What else should I consider when deciding to bring a dog home?

To avoid the unhappy task of finding a new home for your dog, find out whether anyone in your family is allergic to dogs before you bring one home. If you suspect a family member may be allergic to dogs, consult your family doctor to determine the severity of the allergy. If the allergy is mild, find out during your breed research which breeds may be more forgiving than others when it comes to aggravating an allergy.

Are you willing to train a dog?

- You must socialize your dog to accept all the people and situations in your environment.

- You also need to housetrain your dog and teach him basic manners, such as walking on a leash, sitting when asked and coming when called.

- Training your dog will become a large part of your daily routine. Make sure you are prepared to work with your dog consistently.

Can you meet the grooming needs of a dog?

- Some dogs need to be brushed only once a week, while others need daily grooming and regular trips to a professional groomer.

- Regular ear cleaning, nail clipping and bathing are also necessary.

- Also consider how much dog hair you are willing to deal with in your home. Most dogs shed. Dogs with thick, bushy coats tend to shed more than dogs with smooth, curly or wiry coats.

guide to popular dog breeds

Purebred Dogs

A purebred dog is a dog whose mother, father and ancestors are all the same breed.

There is an abundance of information available in books and on the Internet about each dog breed. By researching a breed of interest, you can find out about the adult appearance, size, personality and behavior of dogs of that breed. This information can help you make an informed choice about what kind of dog may be right for you.

Choosing a purebred dog gives you an idea of what your dog may be like, but it is important to remember that each dog is an individual and may display characteristics outside of his breed.

Mixed Breed Dogs

A mixed breed dog is a dog whose parents are different breeds. For example, a Cockapoo has a Cocker Spaniel parent and a Poodle parent. Mixed breed dogs, just like purebred dogs, can make loyal and affectionate pets.

It can be difficult to determine what the adult appearance, size, personality and behavior of a mixed breed dog will be, but his dominant physical features may provide some clues. For example, if he looks a lot like a Poodle, he may grow up with Poodle-like characteristics and personality.

The American Kennel Club

The American Kennel Club (AKC) is a not-for-profit organization that maintains the world's largest registry, or list, of purebred dogs and currently recognizes 153 different breeds. A dog that is registered with the AKC is a purebred dog whose lineage has been recorded for multiple generations. The AKC does not guarantee the health or temperament of the dogs it registers. To find out more about the AKC, you can visit them on the Web at www.akc.org.

The AKC uses seven groups to categorize dog breeds—Sporting, Toy, Terrier, Hound, Working, Herding and Non-Sporting. The groups are based on the jobs the dogs were originally bred to do.

the sporting group

The Sporting group includes dogs originally bred to work with hunters. This group includes retrievers, spaniels, pointers and setters.

Sporting dogs are generally intelligent, friendly and require regular, vigorous exercise.

	Size	Temperament	Grooming	Training & Exercise
Labrador Retriever 	**Height:** 21½-24½ inches **Weight:** 55-80 pounds	Stable, sweet and outgoing. Usually very good with children. First time owners should avoid a dog bred specifically for hunting or field competition.	Short, dense coat requires minimal brushing. Moderate to heavy shedding.	Requires vigorous daily exercise, particularly when young. Due to high energy level, early training classes recommended.
Golden Retriever 	**Height:** 21½-24 inches **Weight:** 55-75 pounds	Stable, reliable and devoted. Usually very good with children. First time owners should avoid a dog bred specifically for hunting or field competition.	Mid-length, dense coat requires moderate brushing. Moderate to heavy shedding.	Requires vigorous daily exercise, particularly when young. Due to high energy level, early training classes recommended.
American Cocker Spaniel 	**Height:** 14-15 inches **Weight:** 24-28 pounds	Friendly and energetic. Usually good with children. When well-bred and well-trained, this dog can make a wonderful family pet.	Medium to long coat requires extensive brushing. Professional grooming required. Moderate shedding.	Requires moderate exercise. Early and ongoing professional training recommended.
German Shorthaired Pointer 	**Height:** 21-25 inches **Weight:** 45-70 pounds	Energetic, friendly and independent. Better with older children. Requires clear and consistent boundaries.	Short, thick coat requires minimal brushing. Moderate shedding.	Requires vigorous daily exercise. Due to high energy level, crating and early training classes recommended.

the toy group

The Toy group includes small, long-lived dogs that were originally bred to be companions for people. Many dogs in the Toy group require only minimal exercise and are ideal for people with limited living space.

	Size	Temperament	Grooming	Training & Exercise
Yorkshire Terrier 	**Height:** 7-9 inches **Weight:** 3-7 pounds	Clever and devoted to owner. Can be barky and snappish if spoiled. Better with older children.	Long, fine coat requires daily brushing. Professional grooming required. Minimal shedding.	Requires moderate exercise. Early and ongoing professional training recommended.
Shih Tzu 	**Height:** 8-11 inches **Weight:** 9-16 pounds	Outgoing, friendly and fun-loving. True companions. Good for first time owners.	Long, dense coat requires daily brushing. Professional grooming required. Minimal shedding.	Requires minimal exercise. Ongoing training provides mental stimulation for this intelligent dog.
Chihuahua 	**Height:** Approximately 5 inches **Weight:** Up to 6 pounds	Intelligent, feisty and devoted to owner. Can be barky, snappish and territorial. Not suitable for children.	Smooth-coated variety requires minimal brushing. Long-coated variety requires moderate brushing. Minimal shedding.	Requires minimal exercise. Early and ongoing socialization is important to avoid behavior problems.
Pug 	**Height:** 10-11 inches **Weight:** 14-18 pounds	Easygoing, playful, charming and even-tempered. Good family pet. Good for first time owners.	Short, smooth coat requires minimal brushing. Heavy shedding.	Requires minimal exercise. Ongoing training provides mental stimulation for this clever dog.

the terrier group

Terriers were originally bred to hunt small animals. Their lively, self-confident personalities make Terriers good watchdogs, but chasing, barking and digging can be a problem for these dogs.

	Size	Temperament	Grooming	Training & Exercise
Miniature Schnauzer 	**Height:** 12-14 inches **Weight:** 13-15 pounds	Active, spirited, self-assured and sensitive. Prone to barking.	Wiry coat requires regular brushing. Professional grooming required. Minimal shedding.	Requires moderate exercise. Training classes recommended.
West Highland White Terrier 	**Height:** 10-11 inches **Weight:** 15-19 pounds	Friendly, lively and playful. Better with older children.	Straight, stiff coat requires brushing several times a week. Professional grooming required. Minimal shedding.	Requires moderate exercise. Training classes recommended.
Scottish Terrier 	**Height:** Approximately 10 inches **Weight:** 18-22 pounds	Feisty, independent and devoted to owner. Better with older children.	Wiry, dense coat requires regular brushing. Professional grooming required. Minimal shedding.	Requires moderate exercise. Early and ongoing socialization and training classes recommended.
Airedale Terrier 	**Height:** Approximately 23 inches **Weight:** 45-50 pounds	Playful, fun-loving, active and protective of owner. A hardy, adaptable dog.	Wiry coat requires weekly brushing. Professional grooming required. Minimal shedding.	Requires plenty of exercise. Early and ongoing socialization and professional training recommended.

the hound group

Hounds were originally bred to hunt by scent or sight. Scenthounds, including the Beagle, Dachshund and Basset Hound, enjoy following their noses. Sighthounds, including the Greyhound and Whippet, enjoy a good run.

	Size	Temperament	Grooming	Training & Exercise
Beagle 	**Height:** 10-15 inches **Weight:** 18-30 pounds	Cheerful and curious. Good with children. Howling, barking and following his nose into trouble can be problems.	Short coat requires minimal brushing. Regular ear care required. Moderate shedding.	Requires plenty of exercise. Early and ongoing training classes recommended.
Dachshund 	**Height:** 5-9 inches **Weight:** 10-32 pounds	Clever, persistent and playful. Digging and barking can be problems. Better with older children.	Long and wire-haired coats require moderate brushing. Smooth coat requires minimal brushing. Minimal to moderate shedding.	Requires minimal to moderate exercise. Early socialization and training classes recommended. Challenge to housetrain.
Basset Hound 	**Height:** 14-15 inches **Weight:** 40-55 pounds	Good-natured, pleasant and sociable. Howling and begging can be problems. Usually good with children.	Short, smooth coat requires minimal brushing. Regular ear care required. Minimal to moderate shedding.	Requires moderate exercise. Food rewards are an especially good training tool for this dog. Challenge to housetrain.
Greyhound 	**Height:** 26-30 inches **Weight:** 60-70 pounds	Gentle, quiet and affectionate. Good family pet. Destructive chewing may be a problem.	Short, smooth coat requires minimal brushing. Minimal shedding.	Requires moderate exercise in a fenced area. This dog requires positive, sensitive training.

the working group

Working dogs are powerful, intelligent dogs who were originally bred to perform a variety of tasks. Working dogs can be great companions for experienced owners who make training and socialization a priority.

	Size	Temperament	Grooming	Training & Exercise
Boxer 	**Height:** 21-25 inches **Weight:** 60-75 pounds	Fun-loving, athletic and courageous. Patient with children. Can be overly exuberant.	Short, smooth coat requires minimal brushing. Minimal to moderate shedding.	Requires plenty of exercise. Early training classes and socialization recommended.
Rottweiler 	**Height:** 22-27 inches **Weight:** 85-115 pounds	Confident, courageous, powerful and protective. May be assertive. When well-bred and well-trained, this dog can be suitable for experienced owners.	Short, dense coat requires regular brushing. Moderate shedding.	Requires plenty of exercise. Early and ongoing socialization and professional training recommended.
Doberman Pinscher 	**Height:** 24-28 inches **Weight:** 60-85 pounds	Loyal, energetic and athletic. A sensitive dog that must be treated in a positive manner. Suitable for experienced owners.	Short, smooth, shiny coat requires minimal brushing. Minimal shedding.	Requires vigorous daily exercise, especially when young. Early and ongoing professional, positive training recommended.
Siberian Husky 	**Height:** 20-23½ inches **Weight:** 35-60 pounds	Good-humored, friendly and outgoing. Destructive digging or chewing a problem if not adequately stimulated.	Mid-length, thick coat requires weekly brushing. Heavy shedding in spring and fall.	Requires vigorous daily exercise in a securely fenced area. Early professional training recommended.

the herding group

Dogs in the Herding group were originally bred to herd livestock. Herding dogs are intelligent, energetic and often independent, but they are prone to barking.

	Size	Temperament	Grooming	Training & Exercise
German Shepherd 	**Height:** 22-26 inches **Weight:** 65-100 pounds	Intelligent, versatile and independent. Thrives when given a job to do. Better suited to an experienced owner.	Mid-length, dense coat requires regular brushing. Heavy shedding in spring and fall.	Requires vigorous daily exercise. Early and ongoing socialization and professional training is required.
Shetland Sheepdog 	**Height:** 13-16 inches **Weight:** 15-20 pounds	Intelligent, playful and devoted to owner. Can be nervous and barky. Better with older children.	Long, dense coat requires regular brushing. Moderate shedding, with heavy shedding in spring and fall.	Requires plenty of exercise. This dog generally excels at obedience and agility training.
Pembroke Welsh Corgi 	**Height:** 10-12 inches **Weight:** 25-30 pounds	Intelligent, friendly and active. Big dog attitude in a small body. Good with children.	Mid-length, thick coat requires brushing several times a week. Sheds heavily.	Requires plenty of exercise. Early training and socialization recommended.
Collie 	**Height:** 22-26 inches **Weight:** 50-75 pounds	Loyal, alert and sensitive. Can be nervous and barky.	Mid-length to long, dense coat requires weekly brushing. Moderate to heavy shedding.	Requires plenty of exercise, especially when young. Early and ongoing training and socialization recommended.

non-sporting group

The Non-Sporting group is made up of dogs that do not fit into any other group. This group contains a wide variety of dogs that differ greatly in appearance and personality.

	Size	Temperament	Grooming	Training & Exercise
Poodle 	**Height in inches:** Under 10 (Toy), 10-15 (Miniature), Over 15 (Standard) **Weight in pounds:** 5-7 (Toy), 14-17 (Miniature), 45-75 (Standard)	Intelligent, dignified and active. Toys and Miniatures are prone to barking. Standards are energetic and make good family pets.	Curly, dense coat requires regular brushing. Professional grooming required. Does not shed.	Toys and Miniatures require moderate exercise. Standards require plenty of exercise. Training classes recommended.
Bulldog 	**Height:** 14-16 inches **Weight:** 40-50 pounds	Easygoing, charming and loyal. Prone to a number of health problems.	Short, smooth coat requires minimal brushing. Skin folds on face require daily cleaning. Minimal shedding.	Requires minimal exercise. Training classes recommended.
Boston Terrier 	**Height:** 12-14 inches **Weight:** 15-25 pounds	Lively, friendly and affectionate. Good family pet.	Short, shiny coat requires minimal brushing. Skin folds on face require regular cleaning. Minimal shedding.	Requires moderate exercise. Early socialization and training classes recommended.
Bichon Frise 	**Height:** 9-12 inches **Weight:** 7-12 pounds	Stable, social and playful. Good for first time owner. Good with children.	Curly, fine coat requires daily brushing. Professional grooming required. Minimal shedding.	Requires moderate exercise. Early socialization and training classes recommended.

where to get a dog

There are many places where you can find a great dog. The type of dog you want will play a part in determining where you should get your dog. For example, if you want a purebred puppy, you should purchase your dog from a reputable breeder. If you want an adult dog, an animal shelter or a rescue group might be a better choice for you.

When looking for a puppy, make sure you choose a reputable breeder who will meet with you and allow you to meet the puppy's parents. To find a breeder who raises the type of dog you are interested in, you can contact the American Kennel Club for a breeder referral service. You can also check the Internet for breed clubs that can direct you to reputable breeders.

If you are interested in obtaining a dog from a rescue group, you can consult with local veterinarians, groomers and dog trainers to find a rescue group in your area. Regardless of where you purchase your dog, you should try to find out as much as possible about your dog's background.

Reputable Breeders

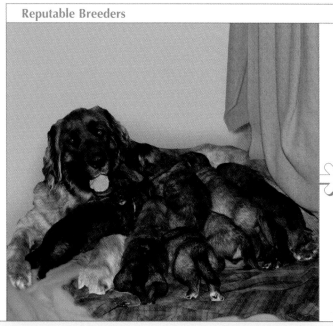

- If you want a purebred puppy, you should contact a reputable breeder who raises the type of dog you are interested in.
- Reputable breeders are very knowledgeable about the type of dog they raise.

- Reputable breeders will be happy to answer questions and provide advice even after you have purchased the puppy.
- Reputable breeders usually keep the puppies inside their home and will encourage you to meet the puppy's parents and other relatives.

- Most reputable breeders carefully interview potential puppy buyers and will usually have you sign a contract specifying the responsibilities of both the breeder and the purchaser.

- A reputable breeder will also provide you with registration papers for your new dog.
- A reputable breeder will always take a dog back if the dog does not work out in your family.

Tip

How will I know if a breeder is not reputable?

There are some breeders who breed dogs only for financial benefit, without regard for the health and welfare of the dogs. Be wary of buying a dog from a breeder who is selling a large number of litters of many different types of dogs for a high price. When buying a puppy, be aware that some non-reputable breeders sell mixed-breed dogs as though they were purebred. Only American Kennel Club registered dogs are considered purebred.

What sources should I avoid?

You should be wary of buying dogs over the Internet, from a classified advertisement or from any other source that does not allow you to meet with the breeder and see the dog's parents.

What should I keep in mind when adopting a dog from a shelter?

Many shelter dogs suffer from anxiety due to being caged, though with love, mental stimulation and exercise, they usually settle down nicely. Since shelter workers work with the dogs daily, they will usually be able to tell you about each dog's personality.

Breed Rescue Groups

Animal Shelters

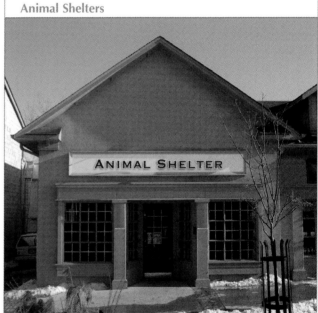

- If you want a dog of a specific breed, a breed rescue group may have the dog for you.

- A breed rescue group cares for unwanted puppies and dogs of a specific breed until a permanent home can be found.

- Rescue workers often work on basic training with the rescued dogs to ensure the dogs will make good pets.

  Note: Any group can call itself a rescue group. You should beware of groups that have a wide variety of breeds of young dogs or puppies available.

- If you want a dog to share your life but you are not set on a particular breed, check out your local animal shelter.

- Many dogs in animal shelters are not there because they have problems, but simply because they did not fit with their previous family.

- Shelter dogs are as likely as any other dog to make happy, reliable family pets.

- You may have to return to the shelter several times until you find the right dog for you and your family.

puppy development

During his first year of life, your puppy will experience several stages of development and will begin to mature physically, mentally and emotionally. The following timeline provides a general idea of how a puppy develops. Depending on the breed of your puppy, he may develop at a different pace.

Birth to 7 Weeks:
Puppy with Mother and Littermates

Your puppy is born blind and deaf, but his eyesight and hearing start to develop between the second and third week of life, about the same time he begins to move around. During the first seven weeks, your puppy should remain with his mother. She uses this period to teach her puppies about social behavior in the dog world, including how to play with others and respect for authority. She also weans her puppies.

7 to 8 Weeks: Your Puppy Comes Home

By this time, your puppy is weaned from his mother and is ready to go to his new home. Between seven and eight weeks of age is the best time to bring your puppy home as he is at a stage where he easily adjusts to change.

Your puppy will need his first set of vaccinations around eight weeks old.

8 to 18 Weeks: Your Puppy and Socialization

During this period, your puppy is like a sponge, absorbing practically everything he observes. To socialize your puppy, expose him to a variety of places, people and situations, but watch for a brief period when he may be easily frightened, usually around eight to ten weeks old. For information on socialization, see pages 72 to 77.

Your puppy is ready to learn some simple obedience commands, such as Sit (page 100) and Come (page 116).

Your puppy will need his second set of vaccinations around 12 weeks old and his third set around 16 weeks old.

4 to 6 Months: Your Puppy Is Growing Up

As active as your puppy was before, his activity level actually increases during this period. To keep him busy, you can increase the frequency and difficulty level of his training. Your puppy still has a lot of physical and emotional maturing to do. His adult teeth begin to come in around this time, so keep a good supply of chew toys on hand.

You should be consistent with your expectations of your puppy and create a comfortable routine that minimizes confusion and stress. Around four months of age, your puppy may go through another phase where he is fearful or shy around new people or situations. As his confidence grows, he will become more independent.

At around six months, check with your veterinarian about spaying or neutering.

6 to 12 Months: Your Puppy's Adolescence

Finally, at around eight months, your puppy's activity level peaks. However, his independence increases and he may begin to test the boundaries of his environment. If this occurs, set up situations where he must earn his life rewards. For information on life rewards, see page 54.

As your puppy enters adolescence, he may start to display behaviors such as jumping up uninvited, begging or pulling on his leash. You should work on correcting these behavior issues promptly and consistently. During this period, keep your puppy in his confinement area when you cannot supervise him. For information on confining your puppy, see page 60.

After 12 Months: Your Puppy Begins Adulthood

Although technically an adult, your dog still has some physical and emotional growing to do. He may be as tall as he is going to get, but his muscle mass may still increase. When he is physically mature, you can start more advanced training, such as agility training. When he is mentally mature, you can prepare him for competitions and tests, such as the Canine Good Citizen® test (page 130).

By this time, your dog is easier to live with. He is comfortable with your family routine and with his place in your home. After his first year, you can limit your vet visits to yearly check-ups unless your dog requires a visit for an illness.

your dog's health and nutrition

As a dog owner, it is your responsibility to keep your dog healthy. Keeping your dog healthy involves taking him to the veterinarian, meeting his exercise needs, feeding him a nutritious diet and keeping him at his optimum weight.

You should take your dog to his veterinarian for annual checkups and for any required vaccinations or treatments. It is important that you feel comfortable with your veterinarian so that you are able to discuss any concerns you have about your dog's health and nutrition.

Exercising your dog regularly will keep your dog healthy and happy. When training your dog, keep in mind that training and exercise are not the same. Even if you train your dog throughout the day, you will still need to exercise him.

When choosing a diet for your dog, make sure you consult with your veterinarian to ensure his nutritional needs are being met. If you feed your dog table scraps in addition to his regular diet, watch for signs of stomach upset and be sure to account for the extra calories to prevent your dog from becoming overweight.

Health Care

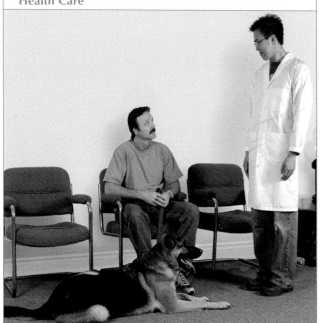

- A healthy dog is alert, inquisitive and ready to train with you.

- You should take your dog to the veterinarian for a checkup once a year. Check with your veterinarian for information on which vaccinations your dog should have and when the vaccinations should be given.

- You should also ask your veterinarian about preventative measures, such as heartworm or parasite prevention, recommended for your dog based on where you live.

Exercise

- All dogs need exercise in order to be healthy and happy.

- If you exercise your dog regularly, he will be less likely to develop behavior problems due to boredom.

- The type and amount of exercise your dog needs depends on your dog.

- You should determine what your dog's exercise needs are and then try to meet his exercise needs as often as possible.

Tip

How can I check my dog's health?

You should do a health check on your dog once a week to make sure he is healthy and prevent problems from going unnoticed. Check your dog's eyes for redness or discharge and pull up his lips to check for red gums. Part your dog's hair to check for skin problems, fleas and ticks. You should also check inside your dog's ears for inflammation, discharge or odor.

How often should I feed my dog?

Dogs over six months old should have two specific meal times per day. You should follow your breeder or veterinarian's advice for feeding a puppy less than six months old. Typically, puppies from three to six months should be fed three meals a day.

If you leave food out all day and allow your dog to eat whenever he chooses, he will not be motivated to work for food treats during training. When your dog knows that you control his meal times, he will pay more attention to you and to the commands you give him.

Nutrition

- There are a variety of feeding options for your dog, such as commercial dog food, home-cooked food or prepared raw diets. You should choose the feeding option that best suits your philosophy and budget.

- You may also choose to feed your dog table scraps in addition to his regular diet. Proteins and cooked vegetables are fine for dogs, but you should avoid giving your dog chocolate, onion, greasy foods and foods with small, sharp bones, such as fish.

- Your dog should be well-fed, but not overweight. When you look at your dog's back from above, you should see an indentation at your dog's waist and no buildup of fat on his ribs.

Note: If you cannot see an indentation at your dog's waist, he is overweight. Check with your veterinarian for weight-loss options for your dog.

the basics of grooming

You should groom your dog on a regular basis to keep him clean and healthy. Grooming your dog involves brushing and bathing, as well as trimming his nails and caring for his teeth. You can groom your dog yourself or take him to a professional groomer.

Your dog will look and feel better when he is groomed regularly. Grooming is useful in the training process, since a dog who is well cared for is often happier and more willing to work with you.

If your dog initially dislikes being groomed, you can distract him with food treats until his comfort level increases. You can then gradually reduce the food rewards and use praise to calm and encourage your dog. Over time, regular grooming will help your dog become comfortable with being touched. This is useful when your dog has to be handled by a veterinarian or professional groomer.

You can find grooming supplies such as combs and brushes designed for dogs at pet supply stores. You can also purchase shampoo designed for dogs, as well as specialized nail clippers.

Brushing

Bathing

- All dogs require brushing to keep their coats looking healthy and shiny. The amount of brushing your dog requires depends on the type of dog you have. Dogs with long, thick coats generally need more brushing than dogs with short coats.

- You should take care when brushing your dog's legs, abdomen and behind his ears. Dogs often have sensitive skin in these areas.

- How often you bathe your dog depends on your dog. If your dog looks dirty or smells, he should have a bath.

  Note: You should brush your dog before bathing him to remove any loose dirt or tangles from his coat.

- You can bathe your dog in a bathtub or a sink. Use a mild dog shampoo, rinse your dog's coat well and avoid getting water in his ears.

  Note: If your dog has long ears, ask your veterinarian or groomer for advice on how to take care of his ears.

Tip

What should I keep in mind when choosing a professional groomer?

To help you find a reputable groomer, you can ask your veterinarian, breeder and other dog owners for recommendations. The groomer you choose should be a member of a professional organization that has a code of ethics. Before taking your dog to the groomer, you should ask whether they use muzzles or tranquilizers and whether you will be able to watch a portion of the grooming. Make sure your dog has had all his vaccinations before visiting a professional groomer, since he will be around other dogs.

What should I watch for while grooming my dog?

Grooming your dog allows you to closely monitor the condition of your dog's body. During weekly grooming sessions, you should run your hands over your dog's body to check for anything unusual that might indicate a health problem. In particular, you should watch for skin problems and injuries, as well as fleas and ticks. If you notice anything that may require medical attention, contact your veterinarian.

Nail Care

Dental Care

- Dogs who walk on hard surfaces, such as pavement, naturally wear down their nails. If your dog spends most of his time on grass or carpet, you may need to trim your dog's nails.

- A dog's nails should be even with the bottom of his paws.

- Trimming your dog's nails once a month is usually adequate.

- Make sure you remove only a short portion of each nail. Cutting the nail too short can cause bleeding.

- Taking care of your dog's teeth regularly can help prevent dental problems for your dog.

- You should brush your dog's teeth at least once per week using a toothbrush and tooth cleanser made for dogs.

Note: Do not use human toothpaste to brush your dog's teeth.

- If tartar builds up on your dog's teeth, your veterinarian can remove the tartar for you.

finding a training class

In addition to working through the training routines covered in this book, there are circumstances in which both you and your dog may benefit from working in a professional training setting. For example, you may not feel comfortable or confident enough to train your dog to perform certain tricks or commands. You may also have specific behavioral challenges with your dog, such as jumping up on people or pulling on a leash, that a training class can help with.

Your dog will benefit from a training classroom experience as well, helping him to be more comfortable with other people and dogs. Remember, though, the goal of a training class is to give you the tools you need to continue to develop your relationship with your dog. A training class is a helpful step in that process.

If you decide to pursue professional training help, be aware that dog training is a self-regulated industry. Limit your prospective choices only to appropriately certified trainers and take time to check references. Sit in on a training session before you select a trainer. You want to feel comfortable with whatever environment you choose.

- A training class may be beneficial to you and your dog.

- A training class introduces your dog to other dogs and people and helps with the socialization process.

- A training class can also help you work through any training related problems you are having with your dog.

- A training class should have no more than twelve dogs and should have at least one instructor or assistant for every four dogs in the class.

- During a training class, the instructor will show you what to do. You will practice each task a few times during the class and then you will be expected to practice at home.

- You should not expect the instructor to train your dog.

Tip

When is it a good idea to consider individual training classes?

If your schedule prevents you from attending a training class on a regular schedule, you can find and hire a private dog trainer to give you and your dog one-on-one lessons. You often have the choice between hosting these individual lessons at your home or taking your dog to a training location. Private training is also a good choice if your dog has specific behavioral challenges, such as aggression toward other dogs, that can be better addressed one on one.

I have tried both group training and individual training, but neither works with my dog. What else can I try?

If your dog has some serious behavioral problems and training is not helping, consider working with a certified animal behaviorist. A board certified animal behaviorist specializes in helping pets and their owners tackle the most severe behavioral challenges. Ask a veterinarian in your area for recommendations.

Questions to ask Yourself

- Is this obedience training designed to help my dog fit into my life so my dog becomes a well-behaved, well-loved member of my family?

- Does the instructor teach positive, dog-friendly training techniques?

- Is the instructor an experienced professional who has experience with my breed?

- Are the demonstrations clear and the instructions easy to follow?

- Are the owners having success with the training techniques?

- Is it fun? Will we enjoy doing our homework as we strive to succeed?

- To find a training class, ask your friends or veterinarian for referrals.

- You should look for a trainer who is a member of a professional dog trainers association or a trainer who has taken the Certification Council for Pet Dog Trainers competency exam.

Note: Dog training is not regulated by the government. Be sure to check the certification and references of any prospective trainer.

- Before deciding on a training class, you should observe at least one class.

- While observing a training class, ask yourself the questions listed above to determine if the class will be a good fit for you and your dog.

your dog and car travel

Whether you are taking your dog on a long car ride or just driving to the veterinarian's office, it is important that your dog be safe and comfortable in your car.

For safety, your dog should either be restrained in a seatbelt harness or confined to his crate while you drive. Properly restraining your dog will help keep him settled and help prevent you from becoming distracted by your dog.

To help your dog become comfortable riding in your car, you should take him for short car rides on a regular basis, starting when he is a puppy. Make sure you take car rides to places your dog enjoys, such as the park or a friend's house. If you only take your dog for a car ride when he needs to go to the veterinarian, he will begin to associate the car with negative experiences.

To help prevent your dog from suffering from car sickness, avoid feeding him for several hours before a trip. Make sure that you always monitor your dog closely for signs of distress while on a car ride.

Dog Safety in the Car

- Keeping your dog properly restrained in your car is safest for your dog, yourself and other passengers in the car.

- Many pet supply stores sell seatbelt harnesses that are specially made to keep dogs properly restrained while riding in a car.

- Make sure that the seatbelt harness you choose fits your dog and has a wide chest strap.

  Note: You should not use a seatbelt harness to restrain a young puppy in a car.

- You can train your dog to sit quietly in his crate when in your car. See page 62 for information on crate training your dog.

- Being in a crate or travel carrier is the safest option for a young puppy when in a car.

- Your dog's crate should be secured inside the car to ensure that the crate will not move in the car.

Tip

Should I allow my dog to ride in the car with his head out of the window?

No. Allowing your dog to put his head out of the window while you are driving is dangerous, since debris from the road may strike your dog or get in his eyes. The danger also exists that your dog could be hit by a vehicle that passes too closely to your car. In addition, your dog's eyes can become dry and irritated due to the wind.

When is it safe to leave my dog in my car?

It is never safe to leave your dog in a parked car. Temperatures inside a parked car can rise rapidly, even with the windows down. While the temperature outside the car may feel cool and the day may be overcast, your car can still become hot enough to harm your dog. Your dog will not be able to cool himself enough by panting in the car and he could even die as a result of overheating.

Getting Comfortable with the Car

Dealing with Car Sickness

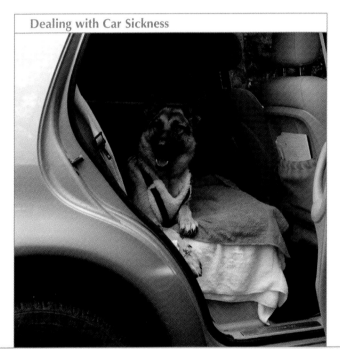

- Start training your dog to be comfortable in the car as early as possible.

- Have your dog sit in a parked car with you. Allow him to explore the car, giving him lots of praise and treats.

- When you begin taking your dog in a moving car, start with short trips and gradually work up to longer drives.

  Note: Make sure your dog is properly restrained in the car before the car moves.

- A dog who drools excessively, vomits or has diarrhea during car rides may be experiencing car sickness caused by the movement of the vehicle or by the dog's fear of riding in the vehicle.

- Avoid feeding your dog for several hours before a trip.

- You may want to place old towels in the area where your dog rides.

  Note: Check with your veterinarian for more information on how to deal with your dog's car sickness.

dog walkers

If you leave your dog at home alone during the day, you can hire a dog walker to take him out for a walk while you are away. Dog walkers are also ideal if you have mobility issues or are unable to exercise your dog properly.

If you have a young puppy that is alone all day, you should choose a dog walker that will come several times a day. Some dog walkers also feed and provide water for dogs, play with them and give them medications when necessary.

When hiring a dog walker, you should make sure that the training method the dog walker uses is consistent with your own. You should also find out how many dogs the dog walker exercises at once. Dogs that are walked in a large group will not be as safe as dogs walked individually or in small groups.

A good dog walker will know canine first aid and will not allow your dog off his leash unless he is in a safely fenced area. A dog walker should also leave you a note after each walk, informing you about the dog's behavior and any issues that need your attention, such as signs of illness.

- A dog walker will come to your home and take your dog for a walk. The dog walker may also provide your dog with food, water and medications when needed.

- Before hiring a dog walker, check the dog walker's references and talk to the dog walker's other clients.

- Try to find a dog walker who walks three or fewer dogs at one time. If the dog walker has a large group of dogs, managing all the dogs may be difficult.

- You should also go on a trial walk with the dog walker and your dog to ensure the dog walker's training methods are similar to your own.

day care
for dogs

If your dog is alone all day while you work, you may want to consider using a dog day care provider. At a dog day care, your dog will be able to spend the day supervised by day care staff while in the company of other dogs.

You can consult with your veterinarian and with your local humane society to find a reputable dog day care in your area. A reputable dog day care will require proof that your dog has been immunized. This is important since your dog will be in contact with other dogs at the day care

and you will want to be sure they have all had their immunizations. The staff at the day care you choose should also know canine first aid.

Before deciding on a day care, make sure the training method used at the day care is consistent with your own. Visit the day care to ensure that you are satisfied with the atmosphere and that the play areas are safe and secure. You should also look for a day care that has scheduled activities, including scheduled play times, meal times and crate times.

- If you work full-time, you may consider day care for your dog.

- Dogs are social creatures, so isolation can cause depression or misbehavior. At a dog day care, your dog can spend his day with other people and dogs while you are away.

- At a dog day care, dogs are taken for walks and allowed to play throughout the day.

- Check with your local animal shelter or veterinarian for day care recommendations.

- Dog day care can help with housetraining and basic training. You should ensure that the day care's training methods and philosophy are similar to your own.

- Look for a day care that has scheduled activities, including play times, meal times and crate times.

- Before deciding on a dog day care, visit the day care so you can determine whether it is the right atmosphere for your dog.

Chapter 2

This chapter will introduce you to the fundamental concepts and techniques involved in positive dog training. Here you will learn how to give a command and tips for effective dog training. You will also find out about the training equipment you will need. In addition, this chapter includes information on how to use rewards during training and the types of training rewards your dog may appreciate.

Positive Dog Training Fundamentals

In this Chapter...

positive training methods

You can use positive training methods to reward your dog when he does something right instead of punishing him when he does something wrong.

When you train your dog using positive reinforcement, your dog learns to associate specific behaviors with receiving a reward. For example, when you say the Sit command and the dog sits, praise him and give him a food treat. With practice, when your dog hears the Sit command, he will be more likely to sit again since he expects food treats and praise.

You can use positive training methods even when your dog is behaving inappropriately. For example, if your dog jumps up on you for attention, give a command that causes your dog to stop what he is doing, such as the Sit command. When your dog obeys your command, praise him for the appropriate behavior. You can also ignore your dog until he stops jumping up and then give him the attention he wants when he is behaving appropriately. In situations where your dog is over-excited, you can positively deal with the behavior by temporarily removing him from the situation.

Positive Reinforcement

- When your dog performs an action and is rewarded for performing the action, he will perform that action again. This is the basis of positive reinforcement in dog training.

- For example, when you say the command "Sit" and your dog sits, you praise him and give him a treat. With practice, when your dog hears the Sit command, he will sit so he can receive the praise and treat again.

Positive Responses to Inappropriate Behavior

Ignore Your Dog

- If your dog is misbehaving to get your attention, the best way to deal with the behavior is to take your attention away from him, or ignore him.

- For example, if your dog jumps up at you when you walk in the door, turn your back on him.

- When your dog stops the inappropriate behavior, give your dog your attention again.

Tip

What should I do if I do not catch my dog in the act of misbehaving?

You should never punish your dog after he has misbehaved, since he will not know what he has done wrong if you do not stop him in the act of misbehaving. For example, if you come home and find that your dog has chewed on your favorite book, do not punish him. Instead, you should take steps to prevent it from happening again, such as making sure your books are out of his reach or placing him in a confined area when you leave the house.

Can I prevent my dog from misbehaving?

You can make sure your dog does not have the opportunity to misbehave by carefully supervising and managing your dog's environment. Supervising your dog will allow you to redirect him before he has a chance to make a mistake. For example, if your dog often jumps up on you when you come home, you can quickly say the Sit command as your dog approaches you so he does not have the chance to jump up.

Give a Command

- If your dog is doing something you do not want him to, give him a command that prevents him from continuing.

- For example, if your dog is digging in your garbage, say the command "Off" and then the command "Come." Your dog cannot come to you and dig at the same time.

- Reward your dog for obeying your command.

Remove Your Dog from the Situation

- If your dog is over-excited, such as playing too roughly with children in the yard, you can place him in his crate for some quiet time.

- Removing your dog from the situation that is causing him to misbehave and placing him in his crate allows him to settle down and keeps him, and others, safe.

tips for effective dog training

To help make your training sessions more effective, you can follow some basic training tips.

Everyone who lives with your dog should be involved in his training, though a responsible person should be in charge. When children are involved in training, ensure they are supervised at all times.

Training sessions should be short and occur frequently throughout the day. Try to incorporate training into your dog's daily routine. For example, practice the Wait command before letting your dog outside. If you use treats as lures or rewards, time your training sessions to occur just before your dog's mealtimes, to ensure he will be hungry.

Training sessions should begin in an environment with few distractions, such as a quiet room in your house. As your dog becomes comfortable with the commands, begin adding distractions, such as having other people in the room.

Avoid training your dog when you have had a bad day or are feeling impatient. You may unintentionally take it out on your dog and make the training session unproductive.

- Everyone who lives with your dog should be involved in the dog's training, but a responsible person should be in charge.

  Note: The person in charge of training must be willing to commit the time required to train your dog.

- Children should be supervised by an adult at all times when working with your dog.

- Every time you are with your dog, it is a potential time to train. You should try to incorporate training into your dog's daily routine. For example, have your dog practice the Sit command before you put down his food bowl.

- You should train your dog for 10 minutes in the morning, 10 minutes in the afternoon and 10 minutes in the evening, for a total of 30 minutes of training sessions per day.

Tip

What should I keep in mind when teaching my dog a command?

As your dog becomes comfortable with a command, you should begin giving the command in a variety of situations. For example, practice the command in different rooms in the house. You can also vary how you give the command, such as saying the command while sitting or standing and giving the command when the dog is to your left and to your right. This will help your dog learn that the command means the same thing no matter where you are or what you are doing.

I have an older dog. Will his age affect how I should train him?

Training your dog will require time and patience, no matter how old he is. An older dog may have a better attention span than a puppy, allowing him to learn faster. When training a re-homed dog, keep in mind that the dog's previous training may cause him to misunderstand some of your commands. For example, if your dog has difficulty with the Come command, you may have to choose a different command word for that action.

- When you begin training your dog, you and your dog should be alone in a quiet room.

- You should train in a room that has as few distractions as possible.

- Removing distractions from your training area makes you the most interesting item in the room so your dog's attention will be on you.

- As your dog becomes more comfortable with commands, start adding distractions.

- With time, you can move your training to other rooms in your house and outdoors with your dog on a leash. When you change the training location, your dog learns that a command means the same thing no matter where he is.

Note: Each time you move to a new location, you may need to go back a few steps in your training.

dog training basics

Training your dog is a fun activity that takes time and patience. To make your training sessions productive and enjoyable, you should follow a few basic guidelines.

When teaching your dog a new command, you should begin by using a lure to guide your dog into the correct position. The lure you use should be an item your dog enjoys, such as a food treat or favorite toy. Using a lure allows you to show your dog what to do without having to use your hand or the leash to push or pull him into position.

Once your dog has begun to respond to a command, you can stop using a lure and continue training using only the voice command and hand signal for the action. You may want to use both the voice command and hand signal, or choose one or the other.

During each training session, you should work on only one or two commands. Begin with a task your dog can perform successfully, and then introduce a new command. You should then end each session with an activity your dog enjoys.

Training with a Lure

- When you first start training your dog to perform a command, you usually use a lure to guide your dog into the position. A lure shows your dog what to do without using your hand or leash to push or pull him into position.

- You will most often use a food treat as a lure.

  Note: If your dog does not respond to treats, you can use another lure, such as a tennis ball or a favorite toy.

- To lure your dog into a position, hold a treat in your hand so that he can see it or smell it. Then use the treat in your hand to lure your dog into the position.

- Your dog will follow the lure into position.

Note: The way you hold the treat in your hand and move the treat when luring your dog will be similar to the hand signal for the command. This introduces your dog to the hand signal for the command.

Tip

I am having trouble teaching my dog a command. What can I do?

If your dog is having trouble learning a command, try breaking the action down into smaller steps and reward your dog for each small success. For example, if your dog is having difficulty with the Down command (page 104), use a treat to lure your dog's head toward the ground and reward that action. You can then work on luring his head and shoulders to the ground for a reward. Continue gradually progressing until your dog is able to move into the Down position.

How will I know when I can move forward in my training?

As general rule, when your dog consistently responds to a command, you can move forward a step in your training. For example, when your dog responds without hesitation each time you lure him into position using a treat, you can begin training using only the voice command and hand signal for the action. If your dog is unsuccessful at the new step after three attempts, you have moved forward too quickly and you should go back to the previous step in your training.

Training after the Lure

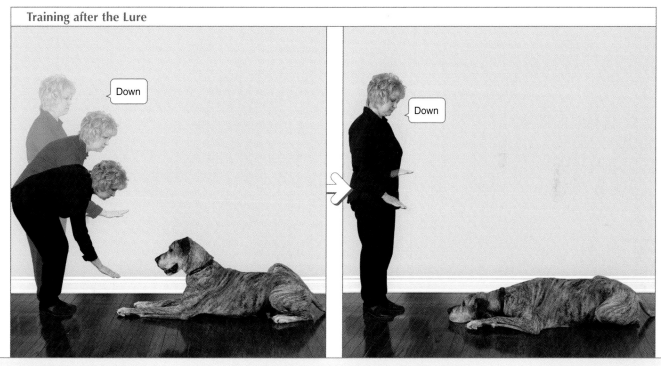

- After your dog responds reliably when lured with a treat, you can stop using the treat to guide your dog. You use a treat only as a reward after your dog performs the command.

- For most commands, you can teach your dog a voice command and a hand signal. When you start training a hand signal, the signal is often a large movement.

- As your dog becomes accustomed to a command and hand signal, you can begin to reduce the hand signal movement until it is as subtle as you would like.

Note: You can use the voice command and hand signal together or use only one or the other.

how to give a command

To help your dog be successful during training, you should follow some simple guidelines when giving him commands.

To avoid confusing your dog, make sure you use each command consistently. For example, you should use the Down command only when you want your dog to lie down. If your dog is lying on the couch and you use the Down command to instruct him to get off, he will not understand what you want and will not be able to obey you.

You should use only one command for each action you want your dog to perform. For example, when you want your dog to sit, say the Sit command. If you tell your dog to "Sit Down" he will not know whether to sit or lie down. Make sure you say each command only once. Saying "sit sit sit" will confuse your dog.

Your tone of voice is also important when giving a command. You should use a calm and confident tone, without changing the pitch or volume of your normal speaking voice. Make sure you do not use a questioning tone or the excited tone that you would use for praise.

Do	Do Not

- Use one command consistently for each action you want your dog to perform. For example, say the "Down" command only when you want your dog to lie down.

- Say the command only once when instructing your dog to perform an action.

- When giving your dog a command, use a calm and confident tone of voice.

- Try to keep the pitch and volume of your voice within your normal speaking range.

- Do not confuse your dog by using the same command for several actions. For example, if you want your dog to lie down when you say the command "Down," do not use the Down command when you want him to get off the furniture.

- Do not repeat the command when instructing your dog to perform an action. For example, do not say "Down down down."

- Do not use a high-pitched or low-pitched voice when giving commands.

setting up for success

You can set your dog up for success by supervising him carefully and creating rewardable moments.

Supervising your dog allows you to help him make correct choices. Your dog will not have the opportunity to misbehave if you are monitoring him closely and preventing unacceptable behavior. Stopping your dog from performing or repeating inappropriate behavior helps your dog to be successful, since it prevents the misbehavior from becoming a habit that will be more difficult to correct later on.

Creating rewardable moments involves finding reasons to reward your dog. Each time your dog makes a good choice or behaves appropriately, you should reward him to reinforce the behavior. This will make your dog more likely to repeat the behavior in the future. When rewarding your dog, use a variety of different rewards. For information on the various types of rewards, see page 52.

Managing your dog's environment helps you create a stronger bond between you and your dog, since it involves focusing on positive behavior instead of constantly reacting to misbehavior.

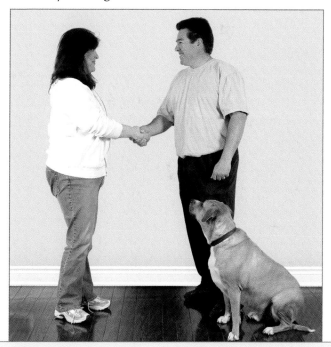

- Supervision is the key to helping your dog make correct choices and preventing him from practicing inappropriate behaviors. You should supervise your dog at all times until he is reliably trained.

- When supervising your dog, attach a long line to your dog's collar. You can step on the line to control your dog's actions, such as jumping on the furniture.

  Note: When you are unable to supervise your dog, place your dog in his crate.

- You should try to create moments when you can reward your dog.

- You should use every possible opportunity to praise and reward your dog for good behavior.

- Make sure you do not take good behavior for granted and only pay attention to misbehavior. For example, when your dog sits politely in front of people instead of jumping on them, remember to reward this good behavior.

training equipment you need

Before you begin training your dog, you will need some basic equipment. To find the equipment that is best suited to your dog, you can consult with professionals such as dog trainers, your dog's breeder, your veterinarian or the sales staff at a pet store.

Toys

Toys are useful for playing games with your dog and can help decrease behavioral problems by giving your dog something fun to do. For example, providing your dog with toys he can chew helps prevent him from chewing household items. A Kong™ is a rubber chew toy you can fill with treats such as cheese or peanut butter. You can also buy your dog stuffed toys, which are ideal for interactive games, such as fetch.

Rewards

During training, you will need items you can use to reward your dog. A reward can be anything your dog enjoys, such as a food item, a favorite toy or a game you play with your dog. Food items are commonly used as rewards during training, since they allow you to quickly reward your dog and then continue working. You should keep rewards in a waist bag or pocket during training so they are easily accessible.

Leash

For training, you should purchase a cotton, canvas or leather leash that is between four feet and six feet long. Leashes that extend and retract are not well-suited to training.

Collar

Your dog will need to wear a collar, even when he is not in training. Make sure you choose a collar that fits your dog properly. You should be able to fit one or two fingers between the collar and your dog's neck. When purchasing a collar for a puppy, choose a buckle or snap collar made of soft leather or nylon. If your dog is able to slip out of his collar, you may want to purchase a limited-slip collar. This type of collar safely tightens around a dog's neck when he pulls back on his leash. Limited-slip collars are sometimes known as martingale or greyhound collars. You should attach an identification tag to your dog's collar in case he gets lost.

Head Halter

If your dog pulls while on his leash, you may want to use a head halter. A head halter fits around a dog's muzzle and neck, and puts pressure on the muzzle when the dog pulls on his leash. Some popular head halters include the Gentle Leader® Headcollar and the Halti Collar.

Body Harness

You can use a body harness if your dog pulls on his leash. A body harness fits around your dog's neck and body. When your dog pulls on his leash, pressure is put on his body. Some body harnesses include the SENSE-ation™ Harness and the Sporn Training™ Halter.

Crate

A crate is a plastic, fiberglass or metal box that has a door you can close. Crates are useful for housetraining and for preventing inappropriate behavior. A crate should be large enough for your dog to stand up, turn around and lie down in.

Mat

You can use a mat or padded dog bed as a place for your dog to lie down and settle comfortably. Make sure the mat you choose is washable and has a rubber backing so it does not slide on the floor.

Exercise Pen

An exercise pen is a foldable fence you can set up indoors or outdoors to give your dog a confined area that he can move around in. Exercise pens are useful for small dogs, but not ideal for larger dogs as they could jump over the pen's fencing. Before placing your dog in an exercise pen, you should remove the dog's collar so he does not become entangled.

Long Line

A long line is a 15 to 30 foot line you can attach to your dog's collar or harness. A long line is useful when training your dog from a distance, since you can move away from the dog while still maintaining control.

You should never leave your dog unsupervised while he is attached to a long line.

types of training
rewards

Using rewards when training your dog helps him to know when he has done well and when you are happy with him. The types of rewards that you can use with your dog include praise, physical contact, food treats, toys and games. Experiment with your dog to determine what he likes most and work with his preferences when giving him rewards.

Rewards are effective because your dog will begin to associate something that he does with a treat. As he learns that he gets something tasty or fun when he performs a command, he will want to do it again,

which helps to make training easy. Training will go even more smoothly if you can time his rewards to the exact moment when he does what you ask of him.

Make sure that you reward your dog with something he likes. If he seems distracted or if he passes up on the reward, he is probably not interested, so move on to another reward. Also, take care when giving out physical contact as a reward. For example, limit it to a quick scratch behind the ears. Anything more will become too distracting.

Praise

Good boy

Food Treats

- When praising your dog, use a happy, upbeat tone of voice.

- You can use a general phrase such as "Good boy" or a phrase specific to a command, such as "Good Sit" when your dog sits on command.

- Praise is often used in combination with other rewards, such as food treats.

- Most dogs also enjoy physical contact as a reward for good work during training. For example, you can quickly scratch behind his ears or on his chest.

- Food treats such as kibble or freeze dried liver are often used as rewards during training because they are easily portable.

- Be creative when choosing food treats for your dog. For example, try hot dog slices, cubes of cheese, pieces of cooked chicken or dry cereal.

Note: Dogs need to lower their heads to chew hard items. When training, try to use soft food treats so your dog can eat them without lowering his head and taking his attention off you.

Tip

Are there food treats that I should avoid giving my dog?

Yes. The two primary foods to avoid are chocolate and onions. Even moderate amounts of these can lead to your dog's death. Check with your veterinarian if you want to try food treats that are beyond the standard hot dog pieces, cheese cubes, apple chunks and so on. Also, if your dog has diarrhea, it may be a sign that his reward food did not agree with him.

What should I do if my dog is not interested in his food treats, even the treats that he normally loves?

Your dog may not be hungry enough to want to work for food. Try timing your dog's training sessions to occur just before his meal time. Also, if he does not finish a meal, make sure that his food bowl is out of reach after his meal time so that he will not just graze all day long. If your dog's reward is kibble, remember to subtract what he eats as a reward from his food bowl so he does not consume too many calories during the day.

Toys

Games

- Giving your dog a favorite toy for a moment of playtime during a training session is a great reward.

- Toys such as rubber bones, tennis balls or stuffed animals are common toy rewards. You should watch your dog when he is playing to determine which toys are his favorites.

- Playing a game with your dog is a great way to reward your dog for good work and to break up your training session.

- You can play games such as Hide and Seek (page 140), Fetch (page 142) or Tug (page 144) with your dog as a training reward.

- Playing games takes the pressure out of training and helps you and your dog strengthen your relationship.

using rewards during training

Rewards are a crucial part of dog training. When your dog receives a reward, he learns that he has done something right and you are happy with his behavior. To ensure your dog understands the correlation between completing a command and receiving praise or a treat, it is important that you always reward your dog immediately after he completes the command. You can use many different items to reward your dog. For information on types of training rewards, see page 52.

When you first start training your dog, you normally use a food treat as a reward after your dog completes a command. As your dog responds more reliably to commands, you can gradually replace food rewards with life rewards. A life reward can be any item or activity that your dog enjoys that is not a food item, such as a walk, a car ride, playing a game or chewing a favorite chew toy. Using life rewards helps you gradually move away from constantly giving your dog food treats for good behavior.

Using Rewards During Training

- Dogs learn by reward association. This means that if your dog performs a task and he is rewarded for it, he will perform the task again.

- For example, if your dog receives praise or food from you when he performs the Sit command, he will usually sit when you say the command, since sitting results in praise or food.

- For best results, you should try to reward your dog at the exact moment your dog performs a task.

- If you are using treats or toys as rewards for your dog, you should keep your rewards handy. For example, you may want to keep your rewards in a fanny pack so you can retrieve them quickly.

Tip

When should I praise my dog?

You should only praise your dog when it is appropriate. If you overuse praise, the impact that praise will have on your dog will lessen with time. Similar to the frequency in which you give treats to your dog, you should only praise your dog when he has earned the attention.

What should be my dog's favorite life reward?

If you play with your dog and control all of the good things in his life, such as food, games and toys, you will become your dog's favorite life reward. To keep your dog's attention, you should constantly vary the type of reward you offer. For example, you can play a game of Fetch one time and then take your dog for a ride in your car the next time.

Using Life Rewards

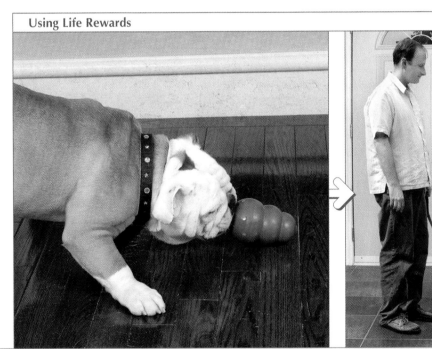

- As your dog starts to respond reliably to commands, you should gradually start replacing food rewards with life rewards. A life reward can be any item or activity your dog enjoys that is not a food item.

- Examples of life rewards include chewing a chew toy, going for a walk and playing in an off-leash park.

- Using life rewards helps you gradually move away from constantly giving your dog food treats for good behavior.

- Even when you are not in a training session, you can have your dog perform tasks to earn life rewards. Earning life rewards allows your dog to do fun things throughout the day.

- For example, if your dog loves going for a walk, have your dog sit before you take him outside for a walk. The walk becomes his reward for sitting when asked.

Chapter 3

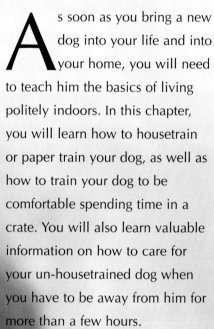

As soon as you bring a new dog into your life and into your home, you will need to teach him the basics of living politely indoors. In this chapter, you will learn how to housetrain or paper train your dog, as well as how to train your dog to be comfortable spending time in a crate. You will also learn valuable information on how to care for your un-housetrained dog when you have to be away from him for more than a few hours.

Housetraining

In this Chapter...

housetraining basics

When you bring a new dog into your home, you should start housetraining as soon as possible. The sooner he is housetrained, the sooner he becomes part of your family, rather than remaining confined to his crate.

The goal of housetraining is to make sure your dog never eliminates inside your home. Instead, you train him to always eliminate in his toilet area outdoors. This means constant supervision on your part so you can get him to the right spot at the right time. When you cannot supervise him, put him in his crate.

Your dog's toilet area should be in a specific area in the yard. Using the same location makes housetraining and cleanup easier. You also do not have to deal with yellow or dead grass, except for in one area.

You should also try to establish consistent feeding and elimination times for your dog, which will reduce the risk of your dog having accidents. Remember to not punish him when he does eliminate in an inappropriate area. Punishing him only teaches him that it makes you angry to see him eliminate, not where he chose to eliminate.

Setting Up a Toilet Area

Sample Schedule For 3 Month Old Dog	
6:30 a.m.	Dog wakes. Outside to toilet area, then supervised playtime.
7:30 a.m.	Breakfast. Outside to toilet area, then into crate.
10:00 a.m.	Outside to toilet area, then supervised playtime.
12:00 p.m.	Lunch. Outside to toilet area, then into crate.
3:00 p.m.	Outside to toilet area, then supervised playtime.
5:00 p.m.	Dinner. Outside to toilet area, then into crate.
7:00 p.m.	Outside to toilet area. Short walk, then supervised playtime.
Before bed	Last trip outside to toilet area.

- You should set up a specific toilet area for your dog in your yard or garden. Having a specific toilet area for your dog will make cleanup easier.

- The area you choose for your dog's toilet area should be separated from the rest of the yard by plants or a small fence. Separating the toilet area from the rest of the yard helps to keep children out of the toilet area and screens the toilet area from view.

- The ground of the toilet area may be completely covered by grass or may have a section of patio stones, pea gravel or sand.

- To make housetraining easier, try to set up a schedule for your dog so you feed him and take him to his toilet area at the same times each day.

- Take your dog to his toilet area when he wakes up in the morning, after every meal, after playtime and before your family goes to bed.

- Your dog should not remain in his crate for more than two hours during housetraining.

  Note: When housetraining, you may find it useful to keep a record of your dog's toileting habits. A written record allows you to see any patterns that are developing and help with the housetraining process.

housetraining commands

The Outside command and the "Do your business" command are both very useful when housetraining your dog.

If you catch your unhousetrained dog in the act of eliminating in an inappropriate place, say the command "Outside" sharply so it startles your dog into stopping what he is doing. Then take him outside as quickly as possible. You should never punish your dog if you catch him in the act of eliminating in an inappropriate place. This will only teach him to hold his bowels and bladder when in your presence and find places to hide while he eliminates, which can make housetraining very difficult.

When housetraining, you can also train your dog to eliminate on command by saying the command "Do your business" as he starts to eliminate in his toilet area. Your dog connects the command with his actions and the reward you give him. Whenever he hears you say those words, he will eliminate to get the reward. The "Do your business" command will come in handy when you want your dog to eliminate before a car ride or before bedtime.

The Outside Command

Outside

The Do Your Business Command

Do your business

1 If you see your dog eliminating in an inappropriate area, say the command "Outside" in a sharp voice.

- The sharp tone of your voice will startle your dog and cause him to stop eliminating.

2 Quickly walk your dog to his toilet area so he can finish eliminating there.

3 When your dog has finished, praise him enthusiastically.

Note: Do not punish your dog for eliminating in an inappropriate area.

- You can train your dog to eliminate on command. This is useful when you do not want to be outdoors for a long time.

1 Each time you take your dog to his toilet area, say the command "Do your business" as soon as he squats.

2 Praise your dog quietly while he eliminates.

3 When your dog has finished, praise him enthusiastically and give him a treat.

- Eventually, your dog will be able to eliminate whenever you say "Do your business."

crate training
basics

A crate is a useful tool, both for housetraining and for preventing unwanted or inappropriate behavior. A crate can also become a safe haven for your dog—somewhere for him to take a nap or enjoy time on his own. Also, going to the vet in a familiar crate helps your dog to be less distressed about treatment and traveling in a familiar crate makes car and airplane travel less stressful.

You can make the crate a more comfortable environment for your dog. For example, a soft, washable blanket in the bottom of the crate provides some padding for your dog, making the crate an inviting place to sleep. Creating this environment is very useful for housetraining because dogs do not want to soil the area where they sleep. For more information on using crates for housetraining, see page 64.

When you are unable to supervise your dog, a crate is a safe place for him to stay and he will not be able to do the things that can get him into trouble, such as chewing furniture or eliminating in the house.

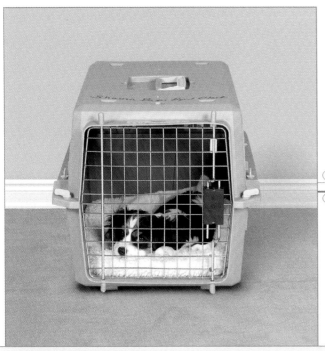

- A crate is a box made of plastic, fiberglass or metal and has a door you can close to keep your dog inside.

- A crate should be large enough for the dog to stand up, turn around and lie down.

- Crates are portable, which makes them ideal for taking your dog to the veterinarian's or for traveling with your dog.

- You can place items in the crate to provide a more comfortable environment for your dog. For example, you may want to put a soft, washable blanket in the bottom of the crate to provide some padding for your dog.

Note: If your dog chews the bedding or blanket, leave the bottom of the crate bare.

- You may also want to include a favorite toy inside the crate. Avoid over-filling the crate with items for your dog.

Tip

What size crate should I have for my puppy?

If you have a puppy and an adult-size crate, you can create a partition to place in the crate to reduce the size of the puppy's sleeping area so that he is less likely to soil the crate. You can gradually move the partition to increase the size of the crate as your puppy grows. If you plan to use the crate for transport or travel, the crate should be an appropriate size to carry and still have room to make your dog comfortable.

Should I use my dog's crate for punishment?

You should never punish your dog while he is in his crate because you want him to have a positive association with his crate. However, placing your dog in his crate as a response to unacceptable behavior, such as nipping your children, is appropriate. The punishment is in taking your dog away from his family and social environment, not in putting him in his crate, which remains a place where he feels safe.

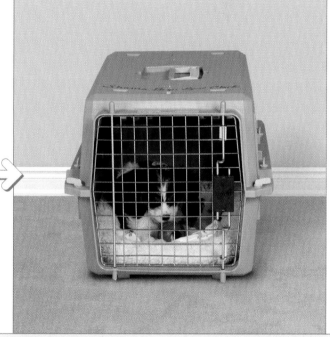

- A crate is a safe place where your dog can go to relax or sleep.
- With training, most dogs will consider moderate lengths of time in the crate to be pleasurable.

- When you are not training your dog to be in the crate, you can leave the crate door open. This allows your dog to enter and leave the crate when he wants to.

- A crate is also a location where you can place your dog to keep him safe when you are unable to supervise him.

  Note: You should always remove your dog's collar before leaving him unsupervised in his crate.

- Crates are ideal for teaching your dog appropriate behavior. For example, if your dog chews inappropriate items, you can place him in his crate with a stuffed Kong™. This allows your dog to satisfy his need to chew in a controlled environment.

crate training your dog

When crate training your dog, you are working to make his crate a place that he associates as happy and comfortable, where he can go to relax and where you can leave him when you cannot supervise him. You work gradually to get him used to his crate, using treats to lure him into the crate and praising and rewarding him for any time he spends quietly in the crate.

You can also reward your dog for being curious about the crate. When he is outside the crate, keep the door open and place goodies inside when he is not looking.

Finding a surprise treat or toy provides a positive association with going inside the crate.

When necessary, an adult dog may be left in his crate for up to six hours during the day or eight hours overnight. For puppies, maximum crate time is their age in months plus one. If your dog is not reliably housetrained and you have to be away for a long period of time, you should set up a long-term confinement area instead of crating your dog. For information on long-term confinement areas, see page 66.

- When your dog has been crate trained, you can leave your dog in the crate when you are unable to supervise him. You must be patient as crate training takes time.

1 Set up the crate and leave the crate door open.

2 Place treats just inside the crate to entice your dog to approach the crate.

3 When your dog approaches the crate to take the treats, praise him.

4 When your dog is comfortable approaching the crate, gradually toss treats further inside the crate so he has to enter the crate to take the treats.

5 When your dog goes inside the crate, praise him.

6 Continue giving your dog treats and praising him as long as he stays inside the crate.

Tip

How do I start crate training my new puppy?

When you bring your new puppy home, try to bring him home early that day so that he has time to get used to being in the crate with the door closed before bedtime. On his first night, place the crate in your bedroom. If he cries, move the crate close to your bed so that you can stick your finger in the crate. The puppy will hear you breathing and know he is not alone.

My dog is barking to get out of the crate. How can I make him be quiet?

If you let him out of his crate while he is barking or whining, you are rewarding him for being noisy. Instead, use a treat to quiet him down before you open the crate door. With a treat in your palm, make a fist, place it against the crate bars and let your dog sniff your hand. This will stop your dog from barking because he cannot sniff and bark at the same time. Count to five while he's sniffing, give him the treat and praise him and then open the door.

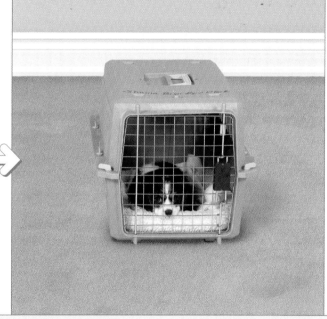

7 When your dog is comfortable being inside the crate for a few moments, gently close the door of the crate.

8 Give the dog a treat, praise him and open the door.

Note: Do not open the door if your dog whines or makes noise. Only open the door when he is quiet.

9 Gradually increase the time that the crate door is closed.

10 When your dog is comfortable with the crate door closed for several minutes, begin leaving the room for short periods.

• Begin by leaving the room for 1 minute, then gradually increase the time you are out of the room.

11 When you re-enter the room, keep your attitude low-key so you do not excite your dog.

Note: If your dog stays quietly in his crate while you are out of the room, give him a treat and praise him before allowing him to leave the crate at the end of the training session.

using a crate for housetraining

Every dog has a natural desire to keep his home clean and not eliminate where he sleeps. Once you have crate trained your dog and he is comfortable with it as a place to sleep, you can begin housetraining using a crate. See page 62 for more information about crate training.

Housetraining teaches your dog to always eliminate outside the house in the location you have chosen for his toilet area.

Puppies should be taken to their toilet area after eating, sleeping, playing or every hour.

Proper crate use helps the puppy learn to "hold it" for longer periods of time because they want to keep their crate clean.

Until your dog is housetrained, he should always be under direct supervision or in his crate. If your dog is not reliably housetrained and you have to be away for more than two and a half hours, you should set up a long-term confinement area for your dog. For more information on long-term confinement areas, see page 66. For every accident-free month, you can increase the size of the confinement area until your dog is reliably housetrained.

1 When housetraining your dog, place your dog in his crate with a chew toy. You can have the crate in the same room with you so your dog does not feel isolated.

2 After your dog has been in the crate for an hour, allow your dog to leave the crate.

Note: If your dog shows signs of needing to eliminate, such as circling or sniffing, allow him to leave the crate before the hour is up and continue with steps 3 to 8.

3 Attach the leash to your dog's collar.

4 Walk quickly with your dog to the outside area you have designated as a toilet area for him.

Note: Walking quickly prevents your dog from eliminating on his way outside.

5 Wait for five minutes for your dog to eliminate.

6 When your dog has finished eliminating, give him a special treat and praise him enthusiastically.

• If your dog does not eliminate after five minutes, walk him back to his crate and leave him inside the crate for another hour. Then repeat steps 3 to 6.

What should I do if I catch my dog eliminating in the wrong spot?

You should never punish your dog if you catch him in the act of eliminating in the wrong spot. This will only teach him to not eliminate where you can see him. He will learn to hold his bowels and bladder when in your presence and find places to hide while he eliminates, which can make housetraining very difficult.

What should I do about housetraining during the night?

Dogs do not eat and drink as often at night and are not as active as during the day, so they don't need to go to the toilet area as often. If your dog is very young, keep his crate close to your bed so you can hear when he cries, indicating that he needs to go out. As your dog matures, he will eventually be able to last through the night without having to eliminate. Until then, when he has to eliminate at night, take him out quickly and quietly so he learns that it is not playtime, placing him right back into his crate.

7 After your dog has eliminated in the toilet area, allow him to play in a very limited area inside the house for approximately 30 minutes.

Note: You must closely supervise your dog during playtime to watch for signs that he needs to go to the toilet area, such as circling and sniffing.

8 After playtime, return your dog to his crate for a rest.

9 Repeat steps 2 to 8 throughout the day.

• Each week, increase the time your dog remains in his crate by 15 minutes until he reaches two hours. You can also increase his playtime by 15 minutes.

housetraining
while you are out

You can housetrain your dog without disrupting your own day-to-day activities, such as being away all day at work or going out for an evening. Long-term confinement is a housetraining method that recognizes the need for your young or unhousetrained dog to eliminate while you are away. This housetraining method allows your dog to not have to eliminate in his crate if he is unable to control his bowels and bladder. In addition, long-term confinement prevents unwanted behavior, such as chewing on furniture.

Although puppies should not be routinely left alone for extended periods of time, if you have to leave your pet alone for an extended period, you can confine him to an area large enough to accommodate his crate, with the door open so he can go in to sleep or chew his toys as he pleases. The confinement area will also have a place for a drinking bowl and a toilet area, such as papers spread on the floor. The confinement area should have a floor that is easy to clean. Also, the area should have little or no furniture or other valuable items that he can chew.

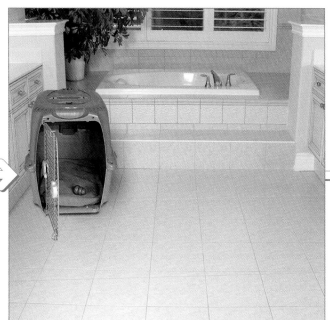

- When you have to leave a young or unhousetrained dog alone for a long period of time, such as when you are away all day at work, you should set up a confinement area for him.

- Confining your dog while you are away for an extended period prevents your dog from eliminating in inappropriate areas in your house and restricts his access to areas where he can get into mischief.

- A confinement area can be any room that has floors that are easy to clean.

- Place your dog's crate in one part of the confinement area. Leave the door of the crate open so your dog can enter and exit the crate as he pleases.

- Setting up your dog's crate in the confinement area gives your dog access to his sleeping area.

- Make sure your dog has appropriate chew toys to play with during your absence.

Tip

I do not have an area suitable for long-term confinement. Are there other options?

If you have a small dog, look for an exercise pen that forms about 16 square feet of confined space. A larger dog could jump over the pen's fencing. Remember to remove your dog's collar before placing him in the pen so he doesn't become entangled.

A better solution is to have a neighbor or friend take your dog out when you are unable to do so. You can even hire a dog walker to do this for you. With this solution, your dog would not be locked up all day. You may also be able to keep clean whatever confinement area he has.

How can I make this training method more effective?

If you have to leave your dog, return home as quickly as possible. For example, if you leave your dog alone all day while you are at work, do not go out for dinner before going home. Also, try to limit how often you confine your dog. Using a confinement area frequently can increase the length of time it takes for your dog to be reliably housetrained.

- Dogs naturally do not want to eliminate in their sleeping area, so if your dog is not yet housetrained, you must set up a toilet area for him to use within the confinement area.

- The toilet area should be in an area away from the dog's crate and water bowl where you can spread papers on the floor.

- When your dog is reliably housetrained, you can gradually increase the size of the confinement area. For example, you can use a baby gate to block off a doorway of a larger room for your dog.

- For each month that your dog does not have any housebreaking accidents and does not exhibit any inappropriate behaviors, you can increase the size of the confinement area.

- Eventually, your dog will be able to be left alone in the house without being confined.

paper training your dog

If you live in a high-rise building or find it difficult to go outside, you may choose to paper train your dog. If you ultimately expect your dog to eliminate outdoors, you should not paper train him.

With paper training, you train your dog to eliminate on newspaper or another absorbent product, such as "piddle pads," which you can purchase at a pet store.

Paper training should always take place in the same location of your home. The location should have a floor that is easy to clean and should be somewhere that disrupts family activity the least.

Until your dog is paper trained, he should always be under direct supervision or in his crate. If your dog is not reliably paper trained and you have to be away for more than two and a half hours, you should set up a long-term confinement area for your dog. For information on long-term confinement areas, see page 66. For every accident-free month, you can increase the size of the confinement area until your dog is reliably paper trained.

- You should set up your dog's toilet area in the corner of a room, such as a bathroom or utility room, that has a floor that is easy to clean.

1 Place a tray or sheet of plastic on the floor where you want to set up your dog's toilet area. The tray or plastic will help protect your floor from damage.

2 Spread several layers of newspaper over the tray or sheet of plastic.

3 Tape down the edges of the newspaper so the paper will not move when your dog walks on the toilet area.

4 When paper training your dog, place your dog in his crate with a chew toy. You can have the crate in the same room with you so your dog does not feel isolated.

5 After your dog has been in the crate for an hour, allow your dog to leave the crate.

Note: If your dog shows signs of needing to eliminate, such as circling or sniffing, allow him to leave the crate before the hour is up and continue with steps 6 to 10.

6 Attach the leash to your dog's collar.

Tip

What can I use to clean up after my dog has accidents?

If your dog has an accident outside his toilet area, first remember that you should not punish him. If the accident has left a stain on your floor, try using a commercial product made from concentrated orange peel. You can also try an odor-and-stain removal product that is specially formulated for pet accidents.

If the reason for your dog's accidents is that he is having trouble targeting the newspaper, rub a bit of urine from the previous clean onto the clean newspaper. The smell of your dog's own urine will help direct him to the correct spot the next time.

I have heard that you can train a dog to use cat litter. Is that true?

Yes. Follow the steps below to train your dog to use a cat litter pan instead of newspaper. Just fill a litter pan with shredded newspaper, cat litter or dog litter. Make sure that you remove any soiled paper or litter after each use and scrub the pan thoroughly once a week to keep it clean.

7 Walk quickly with your dog to the area you have designated as a toilet area for him.

8 Wait for five minutes for your dog to eliminate.

9 When your dog has finished eliminating, give him a special treat and praise him enthusiastically.

• If your dog does not eliminate after five minutes in the toilet area, walk him back to his crate and leave him inside the crate for another hour. Then repeat steps 6 to 9.

10 After your dog has eliminated, he can play under your supervision for 30 minutes. Then return him to his crate.

Note: During playtime, watch for signs that your dog needs to return to the toilet area.

11 Repeat steps 5 to 10 throughout the day.

• Each week, increase the time your dog remains in his crate by 15 minutes until he reaches two hours. You can also increase his playtime by 15 minutes.

Chapter 4

Socialization is one of the most vital aspects of a dog's upbringing and training. In this chapter, you will learn all the basics you need to teach your dog how to accept and deal with everyday life. This chapter covers teaching your dog to accept handling and grooming and to control the strength of his mouth, as well as introducing your dog to other pets, children or a new baby.

Socialization

In this Chapter...

socialization

What is Socialization?

Socialization is the process of introducing your puppy to the world around him. Socializing is a planned training regimen that encourages your puppy to interact with people of all types, other dogs and a variety of situations. In other words, you socialize your dog to accept any person, thing or circumstance that you expect him to respond to positively throughout his life.

Socialization should be one of your first training priorities for your puppy. While it remains a lifelong process for your dog, the majority of his socialization should take place by the time he is 18 weeks old.

The more that you introduce to your puppy during these first critical weeks, the more he will tolerate when he is older.

Unfamiliar people or situations may still frighten him, but as a well-socialized dog, he will be able to calmly and confidently assess and accept whatever crosses his path. When you introduce your dog to the variety that life offers, he will be less fearful, more tolerant of life's inevitable changes and less likely to use inappropriate behavior such as biting when confronted with the unknown.

- Socialization refers to teaching your puppy to be comfortable with a variety of places, situations, people and sounds.

- You should teach your puppy to be comfortable with anything he will be expected to accept as an adult dog.

- Since every family is different, you must make your puppy comfortable with the places, situations, people and sounds he is likely to encounter as a member of your family.

- You should begin socializing your puppy as soon as he comes into your home.

- Although socialization is an ongoing process, the majority of your puppy's socialization should take place while he is younger than 18 weeks.

- Once your puppy is older than 18 weeks, it is not as easy for him to learn to be comfortable when in new situations and meeting new people.

Tip

What are some challenges to socialization that my dog might face?

One potential challenge includes having a new person become a part of your everyday life after socialization has occurred. For example, if you are single, your dog may eventually have to adjust to a new full-time companion in your life. It is impossible to replicate a potential 24-hour relationship with a partner or a child during the socialization process. However, if socialization includes all types of people, your dog may find it easier to accept new people in his life.

If your puppy spends too much time with you and not enough time meeting other people, you may have socialized him too much with you. This problem may result in separation anxiety when your dog is older. For information on separation anxiety, see page 216. Introducing your puppy to many new people will help him be comfortable with a wide range of people.

Another challenge to socialization is when your puppy is well socialized to your children but not to their friends or other children. Again, making sure that your puppy meets many children during socialization should help you avoid this problem.

- Socialization is the key to having a stable, reliable dog and should be the top priority in your early training process.

- The more positive experiences you can provide for your puppy during the socialization period, the more outgoing and confident your dog will be.

- A well-socialized puppy is able to handle new experiences more easily and has fewer fears as an adult.

- A lack of socialization may cause a dog to become fearful of people, other dogs or his environment in general.

- A dog does not need to have a negative experience to be afraid. He may be afraid of anything he was not socialized to as a puppy.

- A puppy that has not been properly socialized may become an unpredictable and fearful dog that displays behavioral problems and cannot be included in all of your family's activities.

CONTINUED...

Socializing Your Puppy

For the socialization process to be successful, you introduce your puppy to a wide variety of people, situations and locations. Anticipate any situation that your puppy may experience as an adult dog and let him experience it before he is 18 weeks old.

Try not to place limits on your puppy's socialization regimen. Bundle him up before he has been vaccinated and carry him around the neighborhood, to the local park, even to work. Expose him to the many sights and sounds of these locations. Introduce him to as many different people as possible, from skateboarders to second graders, from retirees to

newborns. After he has been adequately vaccinated, continue your puppy's socialization on leash, making sure his collar is secure so he does not slip away.

When introducing your puppy to new people, try to anticipate how people will react. You want your puppy to be greeted warmly and treated well so he will mature into an accepting dog. Socialization is most critical during your puppy's first 18 weeks of life, but do not limit his new experiences after that time. As your dog matures, he should continue to meet new people and visit new locations.

- Until your puppy is adequately vaccinated, you must carry him when you take him off your property to protect him from contracting diseases.

- When socializing your puppy, use treats to make your puppy's experiences positive and pleasurable.

- Take your puppy to a wide variety of locations, such as to visit family and friends, to the park or outside a shopping mall, where he will be exposed to new situations, sounds and people.

- Make sure you give your puppy a treat when he is curious and confident in a new place.

Tip

What should I do if my puppy is intimidated about experiencing new things?

Avoid comforting your puppy or otherwise giving attention to his fearful behavior, as this will reinforce the behavior. Instead, try to determine the kinds of situations that trigger this behavior and gradually reintroduce him to those situations, encouraging him for the slightest milestone. Remember also to be generous with your praise and rewards when he responds well to any situation. You want him to have a positive association with anything new.

How can I tell when my puppy has settled down after a fearful experience?

When you introduce your puppy to a situation that frightens him, stand still next to him until he realizes he has nothing to fear. The position of his ears and tail should tell you when he has settled down. A calm puppy holds his ears in a relaxed, half-back position and keeps his tail even with or lower than his spine. He may also wag his tail slowly and gently. When your puppy is relaxed, give him a treat and carry on with what you were doing.

- Socialize your puppy to a wide variety of noises and sounds.

- When you are at home, turn on the stereo or television or run the vacuum cleaner or blender.

- When you are outside, expose your puppy to sounds such as car horns and children yelling as they play.

- Make sure you give your puppy a treat when he does not appear scared of a new noise.

- Socialize your puppy to a wide variety of people, including men, women, children, babies, senior citizens and people in uniform, such as postal workers.

- Your puppy should also meet people who are using or carrying objects, such as people riding bicycles, pushing strollers or carrying umbrellas.

- Try to have each person your puppy meets give him a treat.

CONTINUED...

Socializing Your Puppy (continued)

You socialize your puppy by taking him out into the world to find new people, situations or locations to which you can introduce him. You can also host an event, such as a puppy party, or make use of a training class to create situations during which he has no choice but to meet new people, socialize with other dogs and have new experiences.

After your puppy has shown that he is comfortable meeting new people and trying out new things, you can throw a party for him at home with friendly yet unfamiliar guests of all ages. Hosting a puppy party allows him to meet new people in a familiar and safe environment. He can also experience being the center of attention and being handled by every partygoer, as well as receiving plenty of yummy treats from each guest.

Another structured setting, a puppy training class, is a new environment in which to introduce your puppy to other dogs and their owners. During training, your puppy will play with other puppies and will be handled by the class trainer and other dog owners, enhancing his socialization.

- Hosting a puppy party in your home is another way to introduce your puppy to a variety of new people in a fun and positive way.

- You can invite friends and family to the party—remember to include children of all ages.

  Note: If your puppy is not adequately vaccinated, ask your guests to leave their shoes outside.

- Make sure each guest has a chance to hold your puppy and give him a treat.

- You can also have your guests ask your puppy to sit (page 100) before giving him a treat.

- You should teach young guests how to hold and pet your puppy. Make sure you closely supervise a child who is playing with your puppy.

Tip

What should I do if my puppy is overwhelmed by all the guests at his puppy party?

Do not force him to go to each partygoer. You will only aggravate the situation, making him more frightened and intimidated. This will inevitably set back his socialization regimen, associating large groups of people in his home as a scary thing. Instead, ask your guests to wait quietly on the floor for your puppy to approach them. Gently tossing treats to your puppy may help stimulate his social behavior, but only when he is comfortable enough to want to try a little interaction.

What other things should I introduce to my puppy during socialization?

You want your puppy to feel confident and comfortable whenever he encounters anything unfamiliar. This can include inanimate objects that he may see or feel, especially objects that he will walk on. While walking your puppy around during socialization, have him walk on different kinds of surfaces, such as sand, ceramic tile, wet surfaces, slippery floors and gravel.

- Once your puppy is adequately vaccinated, you can socialize your puppy to other dogs.

- To socialize your puppy to other puppies, you can enroll in a puppy training class. For information on finding a training class, see page 34.

- Attending a puppy training class is a fun way for your puppy to meet new people and play with other puppies in a safe, structured environment.

- To socialize your puppy to older dogs, you can contact friends who have older dogs and set up a play date for your puppy.

- Playing with older dogs can build your puppy's confidence and teach him valuable social lessons.

- Make sure any dog you allow your puppy to play with is healthy, has had all his vaccinations and is stable, reliable and puppy friendly.

handling

You should begin handling your puppy at an early age to familiarize him with having his body touched. Handling your dog regularly will help him become comfortable with being touched by people.

For his health and safety, your puppy will need to be handled for a variety of reasons, including having his nails clipped and during visits to the veterinarian. Veterinarians, groomers and family members will all benefit if your puppy can be touched without struggling to get away or behaving in a threatening manner.

When performing handling exercises with your puppy, you should reward him with food treats and praise after touching each part of his body. This will help your puppy learn to enjoy being handled.

An adult should initially perform handling exercises. Once your puppy becomes comfortable with being touched, you can allow children and other people to perform the exercises with adult supervision to help your puppy become comfortable with different types of people.

- Handling your puppy helps ensure that you or another person can safely touch your puppy's body without him struggling to get away.

- You or a groomer will need to touch your dog to clean his ears, clip his nails, brush him or bathe him.

- You or a veterinarian will need to touch your dog to examine him or give him medications.

- Handling teaches your dog to accept being touched.

- You should perform the following steps from the time you bring your puppy home until he is full grown. When your dog is full grown, you should continue to perform handling exercises.

- An adult should perform the following steps first. Then children can handle the puppy under adult supervision. You should also invite friends to handle your puppy.

- All handling must be done in a loving and caring manner.

Tip

Are there any games I can play with my puppy to help him become comfortable with handling?

The t-shirt game is a fun handling game in which you dress your puppy in a t-shirt and socks. This game helps familiarize your puppy with having his body parts manipulated and prepares your puppy for any future medical treatments that might require him to wear items such as bandages or an Elizabethan collar. An Elizabethan collar is a large, funnel-shaped collar that prevents a dog from licking his wounds.

What should I do if my puppy is uncomfortable with having a particular body part touched?

If your puppy is uncomfortable when you touch a particular body part, such as his paws, nails, mouth or ears, you should proceed slowly and gently while performing handling exercises with the body part. Do not avoid handling the body part or it will always be a source of stress for the dog. Remember to continue rewarding your puppy during the handling exercises, even if the successes seem small.

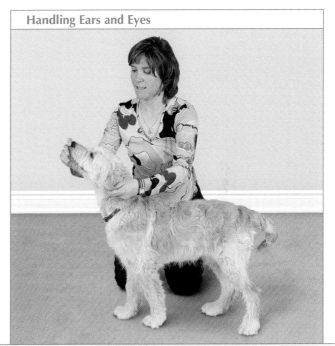

Handling Ears and Eyes

- When first handling your puppy, you will give him a treat after you handle each of his body parts. This ensures that handling is pleasurable for your puppy.

1 Kneel or sit on the floor close to your puppy.

- Your puppy may be sitting or standing throughout the handling exercises.

2 Hold a treat close to your puppy's nose as you perform each of the following handling exercises.

1 Gently touch the area around your puppy's ear or eye.

- If you are handling an ear, you should massage the flap of the ear and gently place one of your knuckles just inside the ear.

2 Give your puppy the treat immediately and praise him.

3 Repeat these steps for the other ear or eye.

CONTINUED...

handling *(continued)*

You should perform handling exercises for each part of your puppy's body, including his ears and eyes, mouth, legs and paws.

To avoid overwhelming your puppy, do not attempt to handle every body part each time you perform handling exercises. Divide the handling exercises into a variety of sessions such as working on the legs and paws during one session and on the ears and eyes at another time.

You can perform handling exercises on top of the dryer to help make your puppy more comfortable when he is on the metal examination table at the veterinarian's office. You can also have a friend your puppy is not familiar with perform a simulated examination.

Over time, performing handling exercises with your puppy will help him relax during grooming sessions and experience less stress when visiting the veterinarian. Continue practicing handling exercises frequently until your puppy reaches adulthood. Then perform handling exercises once every few months to maintain his comfort with being touched.

Handling the Mouth

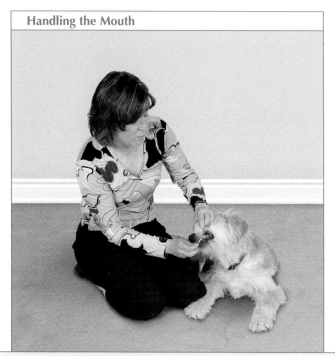

1 Gently touch the area around the outside of your puppy's mouth.

2 Gently open your puppy's mouth.

3 Gently touch your puppy's teeth, gums and tongue.

4 Give your puppy the treat immediately and praise him.

Handling the Body

1 Run your hand gently along your puppy's back, from the top of his head to his hind quarters and then down his tail.

2 Give your puppy the treat immediately and praise him.

3 Repeat these steps, except run your hand along your puppy's front, from his chest to his abdomen and then along each of his sides in step 1.

Tip

What types of treats should I use during handling exercises?

You can use any small food treats your puppy enjoys during handling exercises. If you find it difficult to hold food treats while performing the exercises, you can free up your hands by smearing a bit of peanut butter on the refrigerator door. This will allow you to handle your puppy using both hands while he licks the peanut butter off the fridge. Your puppy will be distracted by the peanut butter instead of focusing on you and becoming anxious about being handled.

Are there any other ways I can help my puppy become comfortable with the veterinarian?

To help your puppy become comfortable at the veterinarian's office, you may want to make an appointment for your puppy to meet the veterinarian without having an examination. This visit should be a positive experience during which the puppy receives food treats and praise. Having the veterinary staff reward your puppy with treats will help your puppy trust the staff and associate visiting the veterinarian's office with a positive experience.

Handling Legs and Paws

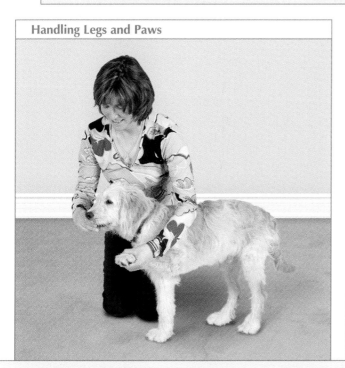

Preparing for a Vet Visit

1 Run your hand gently down your puppy's leg to his paw.

2 Take his paw in your hand.

3 Gently squeeze each of your puppy's toes to extend his nails.

4 Gently touch the area between each toe.

5 Give your puppy the treat immediately and praise him.

6 Repeat these steps for each leg and paw.

• To prepare your puppy for a visit to the veterinarian's office, perform handling exercises while your puppy stands on a dryer. The dryer simulates the veterinarian's metal table.

• You should perform these steps until your puppy is too large to lift. You can also have a friend perform these steps.

1 Place your puppy on top of a dryer.

2 Perform the handling exercises on pages 79 to 81.

bite inhibition

Mouthing and Bite Inhibition

Training bite inhibition teaches your dog to control the strength of his bite. This is important since all dogs may bite when pushed past their comfort level. A dog that has been trained in bite inhibition will cause less damage than one who cannot control his bite.

Puppies begin to learn about bite inhibition through mouthing. Mouthing refers to the natural puppy behavior of play biting and nipping. Young puppies mouth to explore the world, gain attention and encourage other puppies to play with them.

Misunderstandings can occur when puppies mouth people, since owners often think their puppy is misbehaving. It is important to remember that mouthing is a normal and necessary puppy behavior that allows your dog to learn about the strength of his bite.

Puppies have small, sharp teeth and weak jaws. While a puppy bite may hurt, it will rarely cause serious pain or injury. Using your puppy's mouthing behavior to teach him about bite inhibition while he is a puppy helps ensure that serious bites do not occur later.

- Mouthing refers to play biting and nipping by puppies. Mouthing is a natural, normal puppy behavior.

- Puppies younger than 18 weeks have small, sharp teeth, but have weak jaws. Bites from puppies rarely inflict serious pain or injury.

- People often misunderstand why their puppy is mouthing and think the puppy is misbehaving.

- Puppies mouth for many reasons—to learn about their surroundings, to get their owner's attention and to encourage other dogs to play with them.

Tip

When my puppy is mouthing me should I give him a chew toy to redirect his behavior?

You should not give your puppy a chew toy while he is mouthing you, since this will reward his behavior. By giving your puppy a chew toy before he begins to mouth, you may be able to prevent him from mouthing you before he starts. Puppies often mouth at a certain time of day, such as first thing in the morning, or when they are excited. By observing your puppy, you can learn to predict when he is about to mouth and give him a chew toy before he starts.

Should I punish my puppy for mouthing?

You should not overreact to mouthing by punishing your puppy. Punishments such as grabbing your puppy's muzzle or shaking your puppy will only serve to make him scared of you. Punishing a puppy that is mouthing can also make the situation worse by getting him more excited. Instead of punishing your puppy, try the suggestions on pages 84 and 85 for ideas on how to deal with your puppy's mouthing.

- You can use your puppy's mouthing to train your puppy to control his bite and use his mouth softly. This is called bite inhibition.

- Mouthing is not a sign that a puppy will have biting problems when full grown. In fact, a puppy that does not mouth may not have the opportunity to learn bite inhibition.

- Even the most loving and gentle dog may bite in certain circumstances. If your dog should ever bite, an inhibited, or controlled, bite will cause less damage or injury.

- A dog that does not know how to control his bite could use the full force of his jaws to inflict a bite, resulting in serious injury.

CONTINUED...

Training Bite Inhibition

There are several strategies you can use to teach your puppy about bite inhibition. You should start training bite inhibition when your puppy is between 10 and 18 weeks old.

You can teach your puppy that human skin and clothing is very fragile by saying "Ouch" in a stern voice each time he bites you or your clothes. Removing your attention from your puppy for a moment will reinforce that he has done something wrong. Allowing your puppy to play with other puppies and with trusted adult dogs will also help

him learn bite inhibition. When your dog bites another puppy too hard, the other puppy will stop playing with him for a while, teaching your puppy that he has gone too far. When your puppy bites an adult dog too hard, the adult dog may correct him.

You can use meal times to teach your puppy about bite inhibition by hand feeding him a portion of his meals. Each time your puppy's teeth touch your skin during hand feeding, you should remove the food and dish for 30 seconds to show him that he has done something wrong.

- You can teach your puppy that skin and clothing should not be bitten.

1 When your puppy bites your skin or clothing, say "Ouch" in a stern voice. Then stand and turn away from your puppy.

2 After 20 seconds, return your attention to your puppy.

Note: After three bites in a row, have your puppy perform a basic command, such as Sit (page 100). Then reward your puppy's appropriate behavior with a chew toy and place him in his crate for some quiet time.

- Allow your puppy to play with trusted dogs.

- When your puppy bites another puppy, the bitten puppy temporarily stops playing with your puppy. This teaches your puppy that biting results in the loss of a playmate.

- When your puppy bites an older dog, the dog may correct your puppy. This teaches your puppy that biting is an inappropriate behavior.

How can I help my children participate in training bite inhibition?

You can teach your children to play the "Make a Tree" game with your puppy to help teach him bite inhibition. When your puppy starts to mouth your child, have your child stand up and turn away from your puppy. Your child should then tuck their hands under their armpits, put their nose in the air and plant their feet in one spot. This removes your child from your puppy and prevents your child from getting your puppy more excited by waving their arms and running around.

Playing a game makes training your puppy fun for your children and gives them recourse when your puppy nips at them.

How does an adult dog correct a puppy that has bitten him too hard?

An adult dog will occasionally snarl, curl up his lip or growl at the puppy. You should not be too concerned with this type of behavior as adult dogs rarely hurt a puppy when correcting the puppy's behavior. However, make sure that you are very familiar with any adult dogs you allow to interact with your puppy.

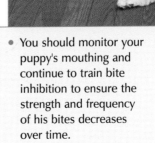

- Hand feeding your puppy a portion of his meal teaches your puppy to use his teeth gently around human hands.

1 Sit on the floor next to your puppy and his food bowl.

2 Take some food out of the bowl.

3 Feed your puppy from your hand.

- If your puppy's teeth touch you at any time, pick up the bowl and put it out of your puppy's reach for 30 seconds.

- You should monitor your puppy's mouthing and continue to train bite inhibition to ensure the strength and frequency of his bites decreases over time.

- Puppies over three months old should mouth with very little jaw pressure.

- Puppies over five months old should not mouth people or clothing.

introducing a new dog to other pets

Bringing a new dog into your home requires some adjustment by every member of your household, especially any pets that are already part of the family. When you introduce a new dog to your existing pets, allow your current pets the time and space they need to adjust to the new dog.

If you already have pets, avoid forcing interaction with the new dog, even when you are supervising. Instead, let your current pets visit with your new dog at their own pace. If you sense that any of your pets are uncomfortable during a visit, you should provide them with an easy escape route.

Before you add another dog to your family, your current dog should be at least one year old. If you have a cat, trim his claws before you bring your new dog home. With time and patience, a relationship will develop between your new dog and current pets. It may be a deep relationship from day one or develop into tolerance over a long period of time.

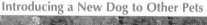

Introducing a New Dog to Other Pets

- Bringing a new dog into your family is an exciting time, even for your other pets.

- To introduce your new dog to a current dog, you will need another person. Both dogs should be on loose leashes and the dogs should meet on neutral territory, such as a park or someone else's backyard.

- Do not force any interaction between the dogs. If either dog seems uncomfortable, allow the dog to walk away.

- Once the dogs are home, you can allow the dogs to get to know each other through a baby gate. The new dog should be gated in his confinement area and the current dog should be free to visit when he wants.

- Using a gate allows your current dog to set the pace of the meetings and to get away from the new dog. This is useful if your current dog is uncomfortable with the new dog or is a much older dog.

Tip

Will my new dog get along with other family pets, such as birds or rodents?

Because these other pets are smaller and more vulnerable, let them set the pace for developing a relationship with your new dog. Until they are comfortable with one another, keep your new dog on a leash for added control. You should also find out whether your new dog has any breed-related tendencies. For example, terriers were originally bred for chasing and catching rodents, so take care when introducing a terrier to a hamster.

My new dog is young and sometimes overexcited. Is this a problem when introducing him to other pets?

Young dogs tend to be short on self control. Your job is to keep a lid on his excitement level when around other pets so no one gets hurt. Do not introduce your new dog to other animals when he is already highly charged, such as right after playing an exciting game of Fetch. Also, avoid leaving your new dog alone with, and able to harass, more vulnerable animals, such as an older dog, a cat or a smaller animal.

Introducing a New Dog to Your Family Cat

- Make sure you greet, feed, treat, leash and pet your current dog first to reinforce his status and help prevent rivalry.

- You should also make sure each dog has his own bed and food bowl and only give bones or other desirable items when you can supervise the dogs.

- Make sure you spend time training your new dog separately from your current dog and socialize your new dog to other dogs outside your home.

- When introducing your new dog to your family cat, allow the cat to set the pace. Do not force any interaction.

- Make sure your cat can get away from your new dog or confine your new dog behind a baby gate.

- Most cats will accept a young dog and will correct the young dog when necessary.

dogs and children

When you introduce a dog into your home, you want him to be a part of your family. Eventually, you want your dog to be comfortable around and even excited to be with your children. Just as you train your dog to be well mannered, your children also need to learn to be responsible dog owners. By following three basic guidelines, you can create a home environment that welcomes positive interaction between your children and your dog.

First, all initial contact between your children and your dog must be under your supervision. If you have small children, never leave them alone with your dog.

Second, your children should respect and treat your dog in the same way you want them to respect and treat their friends. Additionally, if your home is a magnet for other neighborhood kids, limit your new dog's interactions with children to your own. Your kids will have plenty of time later to introduce their dog to their friends.

Finally, designate for your dog a place of his own, such as his crate, that is off limits to your children when he wants to get away.

- Bringing a dog into your family can enrich the lives of all the members of your family.

- To ensure your children and your dog develop a positive relationship, teach your children and dog how to behave around one another.

- If your children have limited experience with dogs, teach them how to be devoted dog owners.

- Children learn from adult behavior. Always treat your dog with compassion and your children will do the same.

- When you first bring a new dog home, a responsible adult should supervise all the interaction between your children and dog. Close supervision ensures that your children and dog safely enjoy each other's company.

- Teach your children to handle your dog kindly and gently at all times. Children should never be allowed to pull your dog's ears or tail. Children also should never chase, sit on, hit, harass or tease your dog in any way.

What breeds are best around children?

Just about any dog can be great with kids, as long as he has been properly trained and has developed strong socializing skills. The obvious exceptions are dogs with severe behavioral problems. You do have some challenges to consider, however, depending on the size of your dog. For example, while larger dogs tend to be more patient with children, they may accidentally knock over a child while playing. On the other hand, smaller dogs may be at risk of having kids fall on them if you do not teach your kids how to behave around them.

How do I introduce an adult dog, such as one from a shelter, to my children?

All the information on these and the following pages applies to adult dogs as well as to puppies. Close supervision is especially important when introducing an adult dog to your family. Until your dog and your children are comfortable with each other, you should use a baby gate to keep them separated when you cannot supervise them.

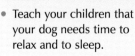

- Teach your children that your dog needs time to relax and to sleep.

- Your children should learn that when your dog goes to his crate or sleeping area, he needs some quiet time and should be left alone.

- If your new dog is a puppy, do not allow your children to pick up and walk around with the puppy. The puppy could get hurt if he falls out of a child's arms.

- Children should sit on the floor to hold your puppy.

- Teach your children not to run or scream around your puppy. This kind of behavior may overly excite your puppy, causing him to mouth or nip the children.

CONTINUED...

dogs and
children *(continued)*

Encouraging Positive Interaction

After you have taught your dog the basics of his training, you can then teach your children how to control your dog. When your children work with your dog on simple exercises or easygoing activities, they both learn how to interact with each other.

Your dog should respond correctly and positively to each member of your family. By allowing your kids to use food treats to reward your dog for some simple routines, your dog's early experiences with your children are sure to be positive. Your dog will learn

to associate the treats with your children's presence, and he will learn that being close to your children is a good place to be.

In addition to working with your dog on simple exercises, some calm games and activities can help your children and your dog get to know one another. These activities can include allowing your children to pet your dog, to brush your dog's coat or to throw some toys that your dog can retrieve.

- You can use treats to help ensure the early experiences your new dog has with your children are positive.

1 Give your child some treats and have the child sit quietly on the floor.

2 Ask your child to gently toss a treat toward your dog.

3 If your dog takes the treat, your child can offer your dog a treat from the palm of her hand.

4 If your dog eats the treat from the palm of your child's hand, your child can gently pet your dog.

5 Repeat steps 1 to 4 with your other children and any children from outside your home.

- Your dog learns to enjoy the company and handling of children and your child learns to handle your dog quietly and gently.

Tip

How should my children act around a dog they do not know?

Teach your children that certain acts that they see as friendly can be interpreted as threatening by a dog, especially one who does not know your children. Running up and hugging a dog, petting a dog on his head and staring into a dog's eyes can make an unfamiliar dog feel threatened.

Should I let my child approach an unfamiliar dog?

Teach your children to always ask permission before approaching an unfamiliar dog. They should ask you (as the parent), the dog's owner and the dog. To ask the dog for permission, they can say the command "Sit." If the dog sits, then he is ready to be approached, perhaps by petting him on his side instead of on his head. If he does not sit, your child should not interact with him.

Can I have my children do further training with my dog?

Kids love to give commands and watch their dog obey. Some training schools encourage the involvement of children, as it ensures your dog will get consistent commands from each family member. For information on finding a training school, see page 34.

- You can also teach your child how to have your new dog sit.

- Your child learns how to use a command to control your dog and your dog learns to sit when greeting a child.

1 Stand with your child in front of your dog.

2 Place a treat in your child's right hand and then cover her right hand with your right hand.

3 Show your child how to lure your dog into the Sit position (page 100).

4 When your dog sits, ask your child to give your dog the treat.

- Once your child understands how to ask your dog to sit, your child should always ask your dog to sit before playing with him.

Note: If your dog does not sit, it could signal your dog is not in the mood to play and your child should leave the dog alone.

5 Repeat steps 1 to 4 with your other children.

preparing your dog for a new baby

Changes in your dog's environment can be very stressful to him. One of the biggest changes that may occur is the introduction of a new baby to his home. If you are expecting a new arrival, you should take steps before and after the baby arrives to manage and minimize your dog's stress.

Your dog will inevitably receive less attention from you after your baby's arrival. You should prepare him for this reality before your baby comes. Gradually give your dog less attention during the pregnancy. It will then be less of a shock when he gets less attention after the baby arrives.

However, you should not ignore your dog completely. Make sure you still give him a reasonable amount of attention.

After your baby arrives, you want your dog to have a positive association with your baby. Continue his same feeding, grooming and exercise schedule, whenever possible. Praise, feed and play with your dog when your baby is around. If he appears depressed around the baby or distressed by the baby's crying, you should not comfort him. You will only reward this behavior, which will encourage him to exhibit stress related behaviors around your baby.

Before the Baby Arrives

- When you are expecting a new baby, there are several things you can do to make the transition as smooth as possible for your dog.

- Practice basic commands. For example, practice the Stay command (page 108) and the "Go to Your Place" command (page 124) so you are not tripping over your dog as you feed, dress or bathe your baby.

- If you are going to change your dog's sleeping area or prevent him from accessing certain rooms, make these changes long before the baby comes home.

- Introduce your dog to children you trust and walk him on a leash around parks so he can become accustomed to seeing and hearing children.

Tip

Is there anything else I can do to prepare my dog for a new baby?

Before you bring your new baby home, take a piece of your baby's clothing home from the hospital for your dog to smell. Make sure you carry that piece of clothing home in a sealed bag. When you take the clothing out of the bag and let your dog smell it, be sure to give him a treat so his first association with the smell is positive.

What other preparations should I make as my baby grows into a toddler?

As your child grows, you want to make sure your dog understands that he is not permitted to touch your child's toys and things. Work with the Off command (page 112) to teach your dog to stay away from your child's toys. You also need to ready your dog for the curiosity of tiny hands.

Continue to practice handling exercises (page 78) to help prepare your dog to be touched and handled by your child. Finally, maintain your close supervision, never leaving your dog and child alone.

When the Baby Comes Home

- To introduce your dog to your new baby, one parent holds the baby while the other parent attaches the leash to the dog's collar and manages the dog.

- Introduce your dog to your baby by allowing the dog to see and smell the baby. You may want to allow your dog to smell only the baby's back or feet. Keep the introduction calm and low key.

- Maintain your dog's feeding, grooming and exercise schedule. This will keep him busy and reduce his stress.

- Give your dog plenty of attention when the baby is present and ignore the dog when the baby is out of the room. This teaches your dog that having the baby around is a good thing.

- **Never leave your dog and baby unsupervised.**

understanding dog
body language

You can determine how your dog is feeling by interpreting his body language. Your dog's body position, facial expression and tail movements all give clues about his mood. Learning to interpret your dog's body language will help you better understand your dog and help you to develop a better relationship with him.

Body Language as a Training Tool

Learning to read your dog's body language is important during training, since understanding his mood allows you to predict his behavior. For example, once you can identify when your dog is feeling a particular way, such as fearful or stressed, you will be able to anticipate possible misbehavior and take steps to keep your dog under control. In particular, knowing when your dog feels stressed or fearful during training will allow you to change the situation and make him feel more comfortable.

Body Language and Unfamiliar Dogs

Since all dogs have subtle differences in mannerisms, you may have difficulty reading the body language of a strange dog. As a rule, you should always be cautious around unfamiliar dogs. Children should never interact with an unfamiliar dog unless they are very closely supervised and the dog's owner is present.

Dogs and Your Body Language

In addition to learning how to interpret your dog's body language, you should also consider the signals you may be giving your dog unintentionally through your own body language. For example, direct eye contact can be threatening to a dog. Your dog may be frightened when you look him in the eye, or he may react with aggression. Bending over your dog can also be seen by your dog as a threatening gesture. Instead, you should try to stand up straight when you are near your dog. If you know your dog well, you may want to squat down and allow him to approach you.

Signs of a Relaxed Dog

A dog who feels calm and relaxed usually shows his feelings by holding his ears in a relaxed, half-back position and allowing his mouth to hang open. A relaxed dog normally holds his tail at the same height or lower than his spine. He will show his friendly mood by wagging his tail slowly and gently below his back.

Keep in mind that all tail wagging is not equal. If a dog is wagging his tail stiffly above his back, this can be a sign of aggression.

Signs of Aggression

An aggressive or threatening dog tries to make himself as large as possible. He moves his weight over his front legs and leans forward. The hair along the back of his neck and spine, called his hackles, may also rise to give him the appearance of being larger than he is. A dog who feels aggressive or threatening may point his ears forward and fix a hard stare on the person or thing that he is feeling aggressive toward. He may also hold his tail upright and wag his tail rapidly, as opposed to the low, gentle tail wagging of a relaxed and friendly dog.

If a dog is displaying these signs of aggression, avoid looking the dog in the eye and walk quietly away from him. For more information on aggression, see pages 220 to 225.

Signs of a Stressed Dog

A dog who feels stressed often furrows his brow, much like humans do when they are stressed or feeling worried. A stressed dog may also position his ears out to the sides and hold his mouth wide open, panting heavily or yawning. You can often clearly see the whites of the eyes of a dog under stress. You should take care when approaching any dog that is exhibiting these signs of stress.

Signs of Fear

A dog who feels fearful may show his fear by trying to make himself as small as possible. He moves his weight over his back legs and often holds his tail low, between his back legs. He may even lie down. A dog experiencing feelings of fear usually avoids eye contact and lays his ears back on his head. You should take care when approaching any dog that is exhibiting these signs of fear.

Chapter 5

All dogs should know at least a few basic obedience commands. In this chapter, you will first learn how to get your dog's attention and how to release him from a command you have given. The chapter then shows you how to teach your dog the most basic obedience commands, including Sit, Down, Stay, Let's Go, Give and Come.

Basic Commands

In this Chapter...

getting your dog's attention

You can say your dog's name to get his attention. This is useful when you want to give your dog a command and he is not already looking at you.

After saying your dog's name, you should praise him as soon as he looks at you and reinforce his attention with a treat. This teaches your dog that each time you call his name, you want him to look at you. It is important that you are not distracted during this exercise so that you can reinforce your dog the instant he responds to his name.

To avoid confusing your dog, you should not overuse your dog's name when interacting with him. Your dog's name should be a signal that you want him to look at you and wait for further instructions.

When training your dog to respond to his name, you should start in an area of low distraction, such as a quiet room in your house. When your dog begins to show progress, you can move to an area of higher distraction, such as the front yard. You should practice this exercise frequently until your dog responds reliably.

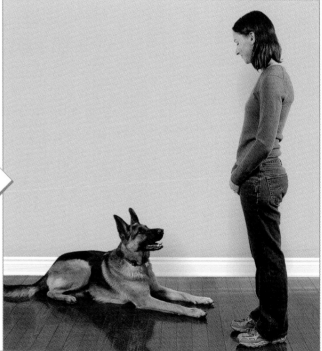

1 Stand close to your dog. Do not stand directly in front of your dog.

2 Say your dog's name once.

3 The instant your dog looks at you, give him a treat and praise him.

• If your dog does not look at you, whistle or make a noise to get his attention. Do not repeat the dog's name. Then perform step 3.

releasing from a command

You can use a release word at the end of a stationary command, such as Stay or Settle, to tell your dog he is now free to move around. A release word lets your dog know that the exercise is finished and he can move out of the position.

Some common release words include "All done," "Well done," "Free" and "Release." You can choose any word or phrase as a release word, including foreign words or phrases and words that are unrelated to dog training, such as "Bagels." You should avoid words that frequently come up in conversation, such as "Okay," and praise words, such as "Good dog," since these words are used too often to be good release words.

Once you say your release word, you should encourage your dog to move around. You can do this by gently clapping your hands a few times, petting your dog, or moving away from your dog so that he follows you. You do not need to give the dog a treat at the release, since his reward is being able to move around.

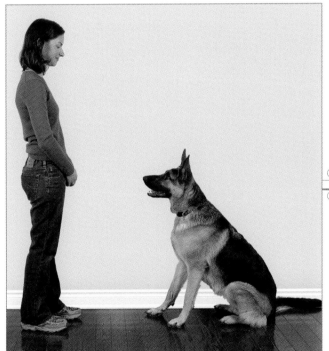

All done

1 Use the Sit command, followed by the Stay command to get your dog into the Sit Stay position. For information on the Sit command, see page 100. For information on the Stay command, see page 108.

2 When your dog has been in the Sit Stay position for five seconds, say the release word you have chosen.

Note: The release word we have chosen for this book is "All done."

3 Encourage your dog to move around.

Note: In this example, we gently clap our hands a few times to encourage the dog to move around.

sit command

The Sit command is one of the first commands a dog should learn. This command is useful for keeping your dog from jumping on people or objects, running away from you or getting into trouble.

When given the Sit command, your dog sits with his hind quarters on the ground. To lure your dog into the sit position without manually positioning your dog, you can encourage him with a treat. When your dog sits, give him the treat immediately.

Once your dog consistently sits when lured by a treat, stop using the treat and use only the command and the hand signal. If your dog does not sit, turn away from your dog for a few seconds and then try again. If he does not sit after three attempts, he may not understand what you want him to do. Go back to luring him with a treat and then try again later without the treat.

Try to practice the Sit command about 25 times a day. You can easily incorporate sit into your everyday routine by having your dog sit before each meal or before he goes out for a walk.

Training with a Lure

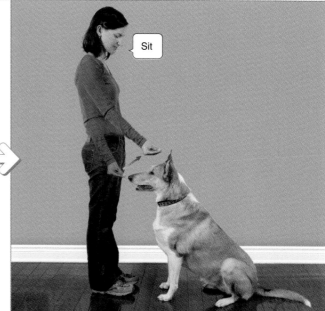

Sit

- When you first start training your dog to sit on command, you use a lure to guide your dog into the Sit position. You will most often use a treat as a lure.

1 Stand up straight in front of your dog.

2 Hold a treat between the index finger, middle finger and thumb of your right hand, with your palm facing your dog.

3 Hold the treat close to your dog's nose.

4 Say the command "Sit."

5 Move the treat up and toward the back of your dog's head.

- As your dog's nose follows the treat, his head will move up and back and his hips will move down.

- Your dog sits.

6 Give your dog the treat immediately and praise him.

Tip

Why does my dog jump up for the treat instead of sitting?

When luring your dog into the Sit position, you may be holding the treat too high or moving your hand around, causing your dog to jump up in an attempt to follow the treat. Make sure you hold the treat close to your dog's nose, even when you are moving the treat up and toward the back of his head in step 5 on page 100.

Where do I go from here?

When your dog reliably sits in response to the command and hand signal, have him sit in different locations around you, not just in front of you. For example, command your dog to sit when he is positioned to your left, to your right, behind you and across the room from you. You can also practice using the verbal command and the hand signal at different times to make sure your dog understands both.

Training after the Lure

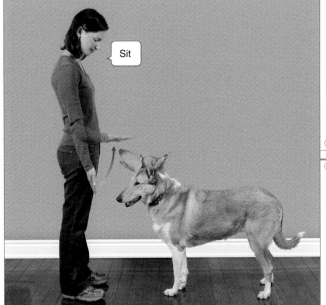

Sit

- After your dog responds reliably when lured with a treat, you can stop using the treat to guide your dog into position. You use a treat only as a reward after your dog performs the Sit command.

1 Stand up straight in front of your dog.

2 Say the command "Sit."

3 With your right hand flat, palm facing your dog, bend your elbow and raise your right hand up to waist height. This is the hand signal for Sit.

- Your dog sits.

4 Give your dog a special food treat and praise him.

Note: If your dog does not sit, turn away from your dog for five seconds and then repeat steps 1 to 4. After three unsuccessful attempts, you should return to training the Sit command with a treat lure.

stand command

The Stand command, along with the Sit and Down commands, is one of the three basic training commands. The Stand command is useful for getting your dog to stand on a scale or a grooming table.

The Stand command includes a verbal "Stand" command and a hand signal. The hand signal consists of positioning your right hand in front of your dog's nose with your palm facing him and then moving your hand slightly away from him. When given this command, your dog should stand still on all four legs. You should reward your dog with a treat only when all four feet are on the floor and he is not moving.

When training the Stand command, keep your body language and attitude low key. Also make sure you do not hold the treat too high or your dog may remain seated. If you want your dog to stand longer, you can allow him to nibble at the treat in your hand before you give him the entire treat.

You should practice giving the Stand command frequently throughout the day, gradually working towards omitting the treat lure and using only the command and hand signal to get your dog to respond.

Training with a Lure

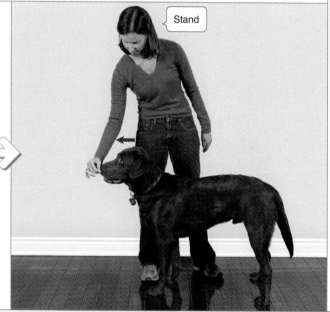

Stand

- When you first start training your dog to stand on command, you use a lure to guide your dog into the Stand position. You will most often use a treat as a lure.

1 Use the Sit command to get your dog into the Sit position (page 100).

2 Stand to the right of your dog, facing his side.

3 Hold a treat between the fingertips and thumb of your right hand, with your palm facing your dog.

4 Hold the treat close to your dog's nose.

5 Say the command "Stand."

6 Move the treat slightly away from your dog, keeping your hand parallel to the floor.

- As your dog's nose follows the treat, your dog stands. Your dog should not walk forward.

7 Give your dog a treat immediately and praise him.

Tip

My dog is having trouble learning the Stand command. What can I do?

A common problem for dogs learning the Stand command is that they tend to walk forward instead of just raising their hind quarters. If this happens when you train your dog to stand, you may be moving your right hand too far away from your dog. You only need to move your hand away an inch or two.

What should I do when my dog learns the Stand command?

Once your dog has learned the three basic commands of Stand, Sit and Down, you should practice these commands with your dog frequently throughout the day. You should vary the order of commands so your dog cannot predict which command will come next. At first, reward your dog each time he changes position and then gradually reduce the rewards until you are only rewarding once for each complete sequence of positions.

Training after the Lure

Stand

- After your dog responds reliably when lured with a treat, you can stop using the treat to guide your dog into position. You use a treat only as a reward after your dog performs the Stand command.

1 Use the Sit command to get your dog to sit.

2 Stand to the right of your dog, facing his side.

3 Say the command "Stand."

4 With your palm facing your dog, move your right hand away from your dog's nose, parallel to the ground. This is the hand signal for Stand.

- Your dog stands, but should not walk forward.

5 Give your dog a special food treat and praise him.

Note: If your dog does not stand, turn away from your dog for five seconds and then repeat steps 1 to 5. After three unsuccessful attempts, you should return to training the Stand command with a treat lure.

down command

Once your dog is responding reliably to the Sit command, you can introduce the Down command. The Down command is useful for calming down your dog when he is very excited or busy.

The Down command includes a verbal "Down" command and a hand signal. When given this command, your dog should drop to the prone position, which involves lying on the abdomen with the back legs tucked under the body, like a sphinx. You should reward your dog only when his elbows and abdomen are on the ground, not when his hind quarters are in the air.

Down is a vulnerable position for dogs and requires confidence and trust between the dog and the owner. In a stressful situation, your dog may be too anxious to comply. Dogs that are assertive, shy or fearful may not respond consistently to the Down command.

You should practice giving the Down command frequently throughout the day, gradually working towards omitting the treat lure and using only the command and hand signal to get your dog to respond. You may still want to reward your dog with a treat for complying with the command.

Training with a Lure

Down

- When you first start training your dog to perform the Down command, you use a lure to guide your dog into the Down position. You will most often use a treat as a lure.

1 Start with your dog in the Sit position (page 100).

2 Hold a treat close to your dog's nose, between the index finger, middle finger and thumb of your right hand, with your palm facing down.

3 Say the command "Down."

4 Lower the treat straight down toward the floor.

- As your dog's nose follows the treat, his abdomen touches the floor and his back legs tuck under his body.

- If your dog does not bring his abdomen to the floor, you may need to move the treat along the floor to lure him into position.

5 Give your dog the treat immediately and praise him.

Tip

My dog is having trouble learning the Down command. What can I do?

Repeat steps 1 to 4 on page 104, making sure you lower the treat slowly in step 4. Keep your hand close to the floor for a moment or two before releasing the treat. You may also need to break the task into smaller, more achievable parts for your dog. For example, use a treat to lure your dog's head toward the ground and then work on luring his head and shoulders to the ground. Gradually progress until your dog is able to move completely into the Down position.

My dog was responding well to the Down command, but now he will not listen. What happened?

Make sure that you only use the Down command to have your dog lie down. If you give your dog the Down command to get off the couch or to stop jumping up on someone, this may confuse your dog. If this is the case, you will need to restart training from the beginning. To increase your dog's motivation and enthusiasm, you may also need to reward more regularly and offer life rewards that your dog likes, such as a belly rub or playtime, instead of food.

Training after the Lure

Down

- After your dog responds reliably when lured with a treat, you can stop using the treat to guide your dog into position. You use a treat only as a reward after your dog performs the Down command.

1 Stand in front of your dog.

2 Say the command "Down."

3 Position your right hand close to your dog's nose. Hold your hand flat, palm facing down and flick your lower arm toward the floor. This is the hand signal for Down.

4 Your dog lies down, with his abdomen touching the floor and his back legs tucked under his body.

5 When your dog lies down, give your dog a special food treat and praise him.

Note: If your dog does not lie down, turn away from your dog for five seconds and then repeat steps 1 to 5. After three unsuccessful attempts, you should return to training the Down command with a treat lure.

settle command

The Settle command is a control command that allows you to direct your dog into a comfortable position when he becomes overly excited. This command allows you to turn your dog "off" when necessary. For example, if children are working your dog up by playing with him, you can tell your dog to "Settle" to calm him down.

This command simply involves a verbal "Settle" command. When you give the Settle command, your dog should move into a lying down position with one hip up. Your dog is also less likely to jump up from the Settle position.

During the training stage, reward your dog with a treat only when you can feel him relax. Then keep him settled with slow petting. You should avoid vigorous petting, as this will work your dog up again.

You should also notice when your dog is naturally settled down during the day and praise him. Keep the praise quiet and low key to avoid exciting your dog.

1 Encourage your dog to become excited by playing with him for 30 to 40 seconds.

2 Remove a treat from your pocket and become very calm and quiet.

3 Hold the treat close to your dog's nose.

4 Say the command "Settle."

Tip

How can I prepare my dog to practice the Settle command?

You can get your dog excited before practicing so you have the opportunity to settle him down.

To get your dog excited, try playing with a toy or touching the sides of his body in a playful manner. If your dog gets too excited and his teeth touch you, you should stop playing immediately. Once your dog is excited, use the Settle command to calm him down again.

My dog gets hyper when we are out for a walk and does not respond to the Settle command. What can I do to calm him and stop his unruly behavior?

When your dog becomes overly excited and does not respond to the Settle command, you can try stepping on his leash to limit his range of movement. Wait until your dog calms down and quietly praise him for his calm behavior. Release your foot from the leash when he has been calm for 5 seconds.

5 Lower the treat straight down toward the floor.

• As your dog's nose follows the treat to the floor, he lies down on the floor.

6 Move the treat slightly to one side to have your dog lie down with one hip up.

Note: You may need to gently press on your dog's hip to encourage him into the Settle position.

7 When your dog is lying on his side, slowly and firmly slide your hand along your dog's body to relax him.

8 When you feel your dog relax, give him the treat and praise him.

9 To release your dog from the Settle position, say "All done."

Note: You can gradually increase the length of time your dog remains in the Settle position.

stay command

The Stay command allows you to control your dog by instructing him to remain in the Sit, Down or Stand position until you give him permission to move.

The Stay command is extremely useful in everyday situations. For example, the Sit Stay command can be used when you want your dog to wait in the car while you open the door. The Down Stay command is useful when you want to prevent your dog from darting into the street. The Stand Stay command is especially handy when grooming your dog.

When your dog can reliably hold a Stay for five seconds, gradually increase the time until he can hold a one-minute Sit Stay, a one-minute Down Stay and a 30-second Stand Stay. You should give treats randomly while your dog holds the Stay. If your dog breaks the Stay more than twice in a row, you are progressing too quickly. You should try going back to shorter Stays.

Incorporating the Stay command into your dog's daily life—about five times a day—will help your dog learn the command. For example, you can have your dog hold a Sit Stay at the door before going for a walk.

- You can use the Stay command to keep your dog in the Sit, Down or Stand position.

1 Place five treats in your right hand and then position your right hand behind your back.

2 Stand in front of your dog.

3 Say the "Sit," "Stand" or "Down" command to get your dog into the desired position. For information on the Sit, Stand or Down command, see page 100, 102 or 104.

4 When your dog is in position, say the command "Stay."

5 Raise your left hand to waist height so your palm is facing your dog. Your hand should be about 6 inches from your dog's nose. This is the hand signal for Stay.

Note: When training a small dog, bend over to ensure your hand is about 6 inches from your dog's nose. Once he reliably responds to the command, you can stand upright.

Tip

How can I reinforce the Stay command?

When your dog can reliably hold a Sit Stay, Down Stay and Stand Stay for 30 seconds, increase the difficulty by adding some distractions, such as stepping back and forth in front of your dog and bending your knees. Then try clapping, bouncing a ball and having other people walk by. Remember to praise your dog and give him treats randomly while he holds the Stay.

Where do I go from here?

Once your dog can reliably hold a one-minute Sit Stay, a one-minute Down Stay and a 30-second Stand Stay with distractions, you can start moving away from him during a stay. Command your dog to stay and move about 6 feet away. Praise your dog while he holds the Stay and walk back to him at random intervals to give a treat. You should never call your dog to you when he is in the Stay position at a distance. He must remain in the Stay position until you return to him. You can gradually increase the distance you move away from your dog until you are sure he will maintain the Stay when you are not nearby.

All done

6 When your dog stays, give him a treat from your right hand. Keep your left hand in the Stay signal.

7 Repeat step 6 for approximately five seconds until all the treats are gone.

● If your dog moves, repeat steps 3 to 7. For example, say the command "Sit" followed quickly by the command "Stay."

8 Lower your left hand down to your side.

9 Say "All done" to release your dog from the Stay.

● Do not give your dog a treat when you release him from the Stay.

● After your dog is responding reliably to the Stay command, you can gradually phase out the treats and start using only the verbal command "Stay" and the hand signal.

let's go command

The "Let's Go" command teaches your dog to walk politely with you outside, without pulling on the leash. When you give the "Let's Go" command, your dog does not need to stay close to your side. He can walk slightly in front of you and explore his surroundings.

Teaching your dog not to pull on the leash is important for your safety, as this prevents him from dragging you along and possibly causing a fall or injury. Your dog also benefits, as you will be more

inclined to take him out if he is well behaved when you go for walks.

When performing the "Let's Go" command, your dog should never be allowed to pull on the leash. Walking at a brisk pace to keep up with your dog will prevent him from getting bored so he won't be tempted to pull on the leash.

You should begin by practicing the "Let's Go" command for one minute several times a day and then progress to longer periods of time.

1 Stand with your dog on your left side.

2 Attach the leash to your dog's collar.

3 Insert the thumb of your right hand through the loop of the leash.

4 Fold the leash into your right hand.

5 While still holding the leash, place your right hand against your stomach.

6 Place a few treats in your left hand and place it over your right hand.

• Make sure the leash is loose. The leash should form a ∪ shape.

Tip

My dog still pulls on the leash when we are walking. What can I do?

There are a couple of strategies you can use to stop your dog from pulling on the leash.

- Stop walking. Dogs pull because pulling successfully gets them where they want to go. If you stop and do not move until the leash is loose, your dog will eventually learn to walk more politely.

- Make a large circle to the left, effectively cutting your dog off before he can pull out in front of you.

Are there any special tools I can use to curb pulling?

Yes. There are several tools you can use to help curb pulling. For example, you can try a head halter, such as the Gentle Leader Headcollar, Halti Collar or Newtrix easyway™ collar. There are also body harnesses you can use, such as the SENSE-ation Harness and the Sporn Training Halter. To find the best tool to help prevent your dog from pulling, you can talk to a dog trainer, your dog's breeder, your veterinarian or the sales staff at a pet store.

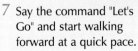

7 Say the command "Let's Go" and start walking forward at a quick pace.

8 When your dog is walking without pulling on the leash, praise him.

Note: When your dog is walking without pulling on the leash, the leash will form a loose ⌣ shape.

9 Whenever your dog looks up at you and is not pulling on the leash, give him a treat from your left hand.

10 If your dog starts pulling on the leash, walk in the opposite direction.

- Your dog turns and tries to catch up with you.

11 When your dog catches up, praise him.

12 Repeat steps 8 to 11 for one minute.

Note: When your dog can walk without pulling on the leash for one minute, you can gradually increase the time.

Off command

The Off command teaches your dog to back away from an item that you do not want him to touch. This command is useful when you want to prevent your dog from eating a piece of food you accidentally drop on the floor or touch something he finds on the ground while you are out for a walk.

You can train the Off command with a treat in your hand or on the floor. When training the Off command using a treat in your hand, do not move your hand away from your dog. The goal is to have your dog back away from your hand when you give the verbal "Off" command.

When training using a treat placed on the floor, always reward your dog with a different treat than the treat on the floor. Otherwise, your dog will expect to be rewarded with the forbidden item when you give the Off command in a real-life situation.

Once your dog responds reliably to the Off command with treats on the floor, you can begin to train the Off command with treats placed throughout the house. You can then move to real-life objects, such as toilet paper and kids toys.

Treat in Your Hand

1 Offer your dog a treat and say "Take it." Then allow him to eat the treat. Repeat two more times.

2 Hold a treat in your right hand, with the back of your hand toward your dog.

3 Say the command "Off."

4 Keep your hand very still. Your dog will attempt to sniff and paw at the treat. Do not move your hand away from your dog.

5 Watch your dog very closely.

6 The instant your dog backs off, say "Take it" and give your dog the treat.

7 Gradually increase the length of time your dog stays off before receiving the treat.

Note: While your dog stays off the treat, you can praise your dog.

Tip

How can I practice the Off command?

To practice the Off command, you can teach your dog the "Cookie On Paw" trick. The "Cookie On Paw" trick also teaches your dog self control. To perform this trick, you place a cookie on top of your dog's front paw and use the Off command to keep your dog from taking the cookie. For more information on the "Cookie On Paw" trick, see page 153.

My dog knows the Off command but does not respond. What can I do?

If your dog knows the Off command but is not responding properly, repeat the command **only once** but in a more growly voice to get your dog's attention.

Treat on the Floor

1 Show your dog a treat and then place the treat on the floor.

2 Slightly cover the treat with your foot.

3 Move your foot to uncover the treat.

4 Say the command "Off."

5 When your dog backs off, praise your dog.

6 Wait for five seconds and then pick up the treat off the floor.

Note: If your dog attempts to get the treat, repeat steps 2 and 4.

7 Say "Take it" and give your dog a different reward.

• Gradually increase the length of time your dog stays off before getting a reward.

give command

The Give command teaches your dog to give you whatever object he has in his mouth. When your dog understands the Give command, he will drop the object he has in his mouth because he knows that when he gives an object to you, he will hopefully receive something better. This command is useful when you want your dog to drop a forbidden object, such as socks or children's toys.

If you do not train the Give command and your dog finds a forbidden object, he may try to play a game of "keep away" with you. Dogs may have difficulties giving up objects they find, so training the Give command can prevent resource guarding issues later on. For information on resource guarding, see page 226.

Once your dog understands the Give command, you do not have to hold a treat to his nose. However, you should always provide him with a reward when he obeys, such as a food treat or tossing the ball with him. Practice this command five times in a training session.

1 When your dog has a toy in his mouth, position your left hand under his mouth.

2 With your right hand, hold a treat close to your dog's nose and say the command "Give."

- Your dog drops the toy into your left hand.

3 Give your dog the treat and praise him.

- If your dog does not drop the toy, repeat step 2 for 10 seconds.

- If after 10 seconds your dog will still not drop the toy, you should repeat steps 1 to 3 with another treat that your dog will want more than the toy.

move command

You can use the Move command to have your dog move aside when he is obstructing your path. For example, if you are carrying bags of groceries and your dog is blocking the doorway, you can tell your dog to move so you can walk inside safely.

You use the verbal Move command in conjunction with a hand signal to indicate the direction you want your dog to move. Teaching your dog the Move command is a useful way to reinforce his status in the household. Between eight and 18 months of age, many adolescent dogs are maturing and they will start to test their limits.

When you first start training with the Move command, you should practice this command several times a week until your dog readily moves when asked. After your dog learns this command, you should make sure you do not step around your dog when he is obstructing your path. To have your dog move out of the way, you should continue to use the Move command. By repeating and reinforcing this command, your dog will learn that he must obey your instructions.

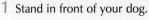

1 Stand in front of your dog.

2 Say the command "Move."

3 With your right hand flat and your palm facing the side, bend your wrist to the right or left to indicate the direction you want the dog to move. This is the hand signal for Move.

- Your dog moves.

4 When your dog moves, give your dog a treat and praise him.

- If your dog does not move, turn away from your dog for five seconds and then repeat steps 1 to 4.

Come command

When your dog hears the verbal "Come" command or sees the hand signal for the Come command, he should leave whatever he is doing and come sit in front of you so that you can touch his collar.

When practicing the Come command with your dog, you should make the experience of coming to you when called the best thing in the world that could happen to your dog. If you need to perform an unpleasant task with your dog, such as clip his nails, give him a bath or scold him, do not use the Come command or your dog will associate the command with a negative experience.

When your dog comes to you, make sure that you touch his collar before giving the food treat. This will prevent playing "chase," which means your dog will come to you, but stay just out of your reach.

You should practice the Come command in a safe environment. After two weeks of consistent success in a low distraction setting indoors, you can practice the command outdoors where you may encounter many distractions, such as people or other animals.

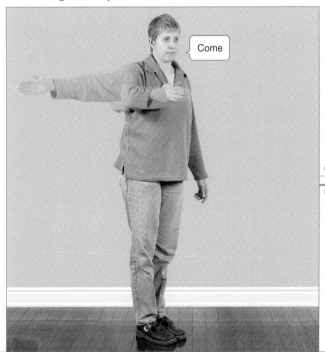

1 Stand within five feet of your dog. Your hands should be at your sides.

2 Say your dog's name once.

3 Say the command "Come."

4 Motion for your dog to Come by making a large, sweeping movement with your right arm, bringing the palm of your right hand to the middle of your chest. This is the hand signal for Come.

5 As soon as your dog looks at you, praise him.

6 Continue praising your dog as he comes toward you.

Tip

Why does my dog not respond to the Come command?

It is possible that your dog has learned to ignore the Come command because he may have learned that the command has negative consequences. He also may not have received rewards for coming to you in the past. You can try training him again with another word instead of Come. You can train using any word as long as your dog gives you the response you want when he hears the word.

What else can I do if my dog does not respond to the Come command?

If your dog will not come when called, you should go to him, making sure that you do not chase him. If your dog runs off when you approach him, turn and run away from him so he chases you. When your dog is near you, take him by the collar and reward him with a treat. Keep repeating this process until your dog responds to the command reliably.

Come and Sit

7 When your dog reaches you, touch his collar.

8 Give your dog a special food treat and praise him enthusiastically.

• After your dog is responding reliably when you call him, you can ask him to sit (page 100) when he comes to you.

1 Use the Come command to call your dog. To do so, perform steps **1** to **6** on page 116.

2 When your dog reaches you, say the command "Sit."

3 When your dog sits, touch his collar, give him a food treat and praise him enthusiastically.

Chapter 6

Once your dog has learned the basic commands, you may want to give him some more advanced training, such as teaching him the Heel or Touch commands. In this chapter, you will also learn how to work distractions into your training to help ensure that your dog will obey your commands in any situation, as well as how to work with your dog on emergency commands that could save his life. This chapter also introduces you to the Canine Good Citizen Test, which you may want to take with your dog once he has learned the commands covered in this book.

Beyond the Basics

In this Chapter...

- Heel Command
- Wait Command
- Touch Command
- Go to Your Place Command
- Training with Distractions
- Emergency Commands
- Canine Good Citizen Test

heel command

You can use the Heel command if you want your dog to pay close attention, such as when crossing the street, in a crowd or when passing an older person or another animal. Before learning the Heel command, you and your dog should learn the "Let's Go" command. For information on the "Let's Go" command, see page 110.

When you use the Heel command, your dog will walk close to your left side, with his ear lined up with the side seam of your pants and his attention focused on you. When you stop walking, your dog will automatically sit, which is an important part of the Heel command.

You can start training the Heel command by using a treat lure to guide your dog. Once your dog consistently heels when lured by a treat, you can stop using the treat and use only the command. To keep your dog's attention when you are not using a lure, randomly give treats or ask your dog to sit while heeling.

You should practice the Heel command for one minute a few times each day, keeping the training sessions brief and interesting so your dog does not get bored.

Training with a Lure

Step 3

Heel

- When you start training your dog to heel, you use a lure to guide your dog into position. You will most often use a treat as a lure.

1 Stand with your dog on your left side.

2 Attach the leash to your dog's collar.

3 Insert the thumb of your right hand through the loop of the leash and then fold the leash into your right hand. Then place your right hand against your stomach.

- Make sure the leash is loose and forms a ⎩ shape.

4 Make sure your dog is close to your left leg and your dog's ear is lined up with the side seam of your pants.

5 With your left hand, hold a treat close to your dog's nose.

6 Say the command "Heel" and then take three steps forward with your dog.

Note: As your dog becomes comfortable with the Heel command, you can gradually increase the number of steps you take.

Tip

How can I keep my dog's attention when training with the lure?

Once your dog is reliably heeling with the treat lure at his nose, perform steps 1 to 8 starting on page 120, except in step 5, move the treat lure up to your waist. When your dog is heeling well with the treat at your waist, randomly move your left hand up to your shoulder and down to your waist and then back to your dog's nose as you walk. Moving the treat not only keeps your dog's attention, but is the first step in phasing out the lure.

My dog is lunging ahead and pulling on the leash. What should I do?

If your dog starts pulling ahead, stop walking forward immediately. Call your dog's name and start walking backwards a few steps. When your dog returns to your left side, you can say the command "Heel" and start walking forward again.

Training after the Lure

Step 3

7 Say the command "Sit."

• Your dog sits.

8 Give your dog the treat and praise him.

• After your dog responds reliably when lured with a treat, you can stop using the treat to guide your dog into position. You use a treat only as a reward after your dog performs the command.

1 Perform steps 1 to 4 on page 120.

2 Say the command "Heel" and then take five steps forward with your dog.

3 Say the command "Sit."

4 When your dog sits, give him a special food treat and praise him.

wait command

The Wait command tells your dog that he should stay where he is and wait for another command. This is useful when you want your dog to wait for you before moving into another area. For example, when your dog reaches a corner before you while on a walk, you can use the Wait command to prevent him from stepping off the curb before you get there.

When you give your dog the Wait command, he does not need to stand perfectly still, but he should not move away from the area he is in. The Wait command is most often followed by the Come command or the "Let's Go" command. When you are ready for your dog to move again, you can use one of these commands to release him from the Wait command.

Before your dog can be successful with the Wait command, he must have self-control. Your dog should already know the Stay command and be able to perform the "Cookie On Paw" trick before you train the Wait command. For information on the Stay command, see page 108. For information on the "Cookie On Paw" trick, see page 153.

- The Wait command tells your dog to stay put until you give him another command.

1 Stand with your dog on your left side, facing the same direction as your dog.

2 Say the command "Wait."

3 With your left hand at your side, your palm facing back and your fingers pointing down, wave your left hand in front of your dog. This is the hand signal for Wait.

4 Walk three steps away from your dog and then turn to face him.

- If your dog moves toward you, repeat the command "Wait" and continue walking.

Note: If your dog moves again, stand beside your dog for 20 seconds. Then repeat steps 2 to 4, taking fewer steps in step 4.

5 Pause and then say another command. In this example we use the command "Come."

- When your dog comes to you, give him a treat and praise him.

Note: You can gradually increase the number of steps you take.

touch command

The Touch command teaches your dog to touch a target, such as your hand, with his nose. This command is useful for keeping your dog safe and close to you when you are out in public.

Considering that dogs usually enjoy performing the Touch command, you can use this command to help reinforce other commands, such as heeling. For more information on heeling, see page 120. For example, when walking down the street and a group of children approach you and your dog, you can have your dog touch your hand and continue with the heel command. This prevents your dog from interacting with the children and makes him focus his attention on you.

Your dog may start to look at your left hand, which holds the treats, instead of touching your right hand. If this is the case, slowly tuck your left hand behind your right hand to achieve the appropriate response. Then move your left hand behind your back again and continue with training.

You should try to practice the Touch command eight times per training session.

Touch

1 Hold some treats in your left hand and then gently rub your hands together to transfer some of the treat smell onto your right hand.

2 Stand in front of your dog, with your left hand behind your back.

3 With the fingers of your right hand together, your palm flat and facing your dog, position your hand approximately 4 inches away from your dog's nose.

4 Say the command "Touch."

5 Make sure you watch your right hand instead of watching the dog. The dog will investigate your right hand.

6 When your dog touches your right hand with his nose, praise your dog and give him a treat with your left hand.

• When your dog starts to reliably respond to the Touch command, you can move your hand to a different location. For example, you can move your right hand closer to the ground.

go to your place command

You can use the "Go to your place" command to send your dog to a specific location, such as a favorite mat, where he will remain until you release him. You can replace the word "place" with any word that works for you, such as "mat" or "crate." This command gives you control of your dog during situations when you need him to be kept in check, such as when you have guests and you want your dog to leave them alone until they are ready to greet him. You can even use this command when you and your dog are guests at someone else's home, if his "place" is portable, such as a mat.

You combine the "Go to your place" verbal command with a sweeping hand motion, pointing to the desired location. This hand signal helps your dog learn that he can go to his place from any orientation. When you work at the command from different positions around his place, you teach your dog that he can approach his place from different directions. After he is responding reliably from these positions, you can gradually increase your distance from his place and also introduce distractions.

Training with a Lure

Go to your place

- When you first start training your dog to "Go to your place," you use a lure to encourage your dog to go to the location you specify. You will most often use a treat as a lure.

1 Stand next to your dog's shoulder, close to where you want him to go.

2 Holding a treat in your right hand, show the treat to your dog.

3 Say the command, "Go to your place."

4 Toss the treat to the location where you want your dog to go.

5 As soon as your dog's paws touch the location, praise him and allow him to take the treat.

6 After five seconds, release your dog by saying "All done."

7 Repeat steps 1 to 6 several times per day for three to four days, making sure you work from different positions around the location.

Tip

What can I do to help my dog approach his place on his own?

When not actively training this command and when your dog is not looking, randomly put a treat on his place without saying anything. Your dog will eventually wander past his place and find the treat on his own. This positive association encourages your dog to start checking his "magic place" for more goodies.

How do I train my dog to use his place to sit or rest?

When your dog is responding reliably without a treat lure, you can ask for a sit when your dog goes to his place. For more information on the Sit command, see page 100.

Start with two rewards, one for going to his place and one for sitting, and gradually get rid of the reward for going to his place, leaving one treat for sitting. Then you can work up to an automatic sit when he goes to his place, which deserves a special reward.

Training after the Lure

Go to your place

- After your dog responds reliably when lured with a treat, you can stop using the treat to lure him to the location. You use a treat only as a reward after your dog performs this command.

1 Place a treat where you want your dog to go, without him noticing.

2 Stand next to your dog's shoulder, close to the location.

3 Say the command, "Go to your place."

4 Swing your right arm and point to the location.

5 As soon as your dog's paws touch the location, praise him and allow him to take the treat.

6 After five seconds, release your dog by saying "All done."

- After your dog is consistently going to the location, you can train without first placing a treat there. Give your dog a treat and praise him each time he goes to the location on command.

training with distractions

When you begin training your dog, you should do so in an environment that has few distractions. A good place to hold your first training sessions is in a quiet room in your house with only you and your dog present. As your dog begins to respond reliably to commands, you should modify the training environment to introduce distractions. The goal is for your dog to continue responding to your commands, even when surrounded by other people, different sounds and more interesting things to see.

While you want your dog to be able to perform any command when distracted, the two most critical are the safety commands of Stay and Come. When your dog reliably responds to these commands even with distractions, the likelihood of him remaining safe in a hectic environment increases.

You should start your training with simple distractions and gradually work up to bigger distractions. Training with distractions does not teach your dog how not to be distracted. You are teaching your dog to pay attention to you, even when something more interesting may be nearby.

Adding Visual Distractions

1 Use the Sit command (page 100) followed by the Stay command (page 108) to have your dog sit and stay.

2 To add a visual distraction, squat down in front of your dog.

Note: Other examples of visual distractions include stepping from side to side or doing jumping jacks while your dog stays in position.

3 When your dog remains in the sit position, give him a treat.

- If your dog moves out of the sit position, say "Sit" and "Stay" again with more emphasis. When your dog complies, praise him. Wait a few seconds and then give him a treat while he stays in position.

Note: If your dog is distracted three times in a row, return to training with fewer distractions.

Tip

Does my dog's breed provide any clues for what objects or sounds may most distract him?

Yes. The activities that dogs were originally bred to do affect the way these dogs react to particular types of distractions. For example, dogs that were originally bred for following scents, such as Beagles and Bloodhounds, are likely to be more distracted by strong scents than by visual or sound distractions. Sighthounds, such as Greyhounds and Whippets, which were originally bred for spotting and chasing objects at a distance, may be easily distracted by moving items they can see far from where you are training.

Guarding breeds, such as Boxers and Rottweilers, were originally bred to keep an eye on the comings and goings of their environment, so these dogs tend to pay more attention to visual distractions around them. Some dogs, especially those originally bred for herding, such as German Shepherds and Collies, are more sensitive to sound than other breeds. These dogs are likely to have more trouble when you add sound distractions to their training.

Adding Sound Distractions

1 Stand several feet away from your dog. Have a helper stand between you and your dog, slightly off to one side.

2 Use the Come command (page 116) to call your dog to you.

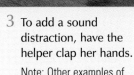

3 To add a sound distraction, have the helper clap her hands.

Note: Other examples of sound distractions include playing loud music or having a helper sing or blow a whistle.

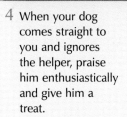

4 When your dog comes straight to you and ignores the helper, praise him enthusiastically and give him a treat.

• If your dog goes toward the helper, say his name to interrupt him. Then say "Come" again with more emphasis. As soon as your dog looks at you, praise him to encourage him to come to you.

Note: If your dog is distracted three times in a row, return to training with fewer distractions.

emergency commands

No matter how well you train your dog, your dog could get away from you and place himself in a potentially dangerous situation, such as walking toward a busy street or chasing an unfamiliar dog. For these types of situations, you should have two emergency commands that your dog responds to reliably.

One of your emergency commands should immobilize your dog so he does not approach a threatening situation. This gives you the opportunity to go to your dog and bring him to safety. The Sit command is a good immobilizing command. The command stops your dog from moving and is part of his early training.

The other emergency command you need is a recall command, such as the Here command, that you can use to have your dog come instantly and directly to you. The Here command is also known as the Really Reliable Recall and is attributed to Leslie Nelson, a gifted trainer with the Tails-U-Win!® dog training school in Manchester, Connecticut. To ensure the effectiveness of the Here command, never use it for anything your dog may consider negative, such as clipping his toenails, or even neutral, such as coming inside after playing.

Reliable Sit

- The Sit command works well as an emergency command because it stops your dog where he is, preventing him from moving closer to danger.

- To ensure your dog will respond reliably to the Sit command under any circumstance, give the Sit command while you are in a variety of postures, such as sitting in a chair, lying on the floor or standing with your back turned to your dog.

- When your dog responds reliably to the Sit command given from a variety of postures, practice the Sit command in a variety of distracting situations, such as outside with other animals nearby, at a soccer game or outside a school at pick-up time.

- Continue to practice in distracting situations until you know your dog will respond to the Sit command when faced with distractions.

Tip

How does training the Here command differ from training commands that I use more regularly?

You should train the Here command three times per day only. You should also train the command in a low distraction area and only give the command when you are sure your dog will come to you. Use a special food treat, such as roast beef or peanut butter, for training this command.

When your dog reliably responds to the Here command indoors—usually after two weeks—take him outside to a fenced location, with a 15 to 20 foot long line attached to his collar. The line lets you control your dog, but is not as confining as a leash. Tie a few knots in the end of the line and let your dog drag the line while he plays. If your dog does not come after you say the Here command once, step on his line. When he turns or starts toward you, praise him enthusiastically. Reserve your special food reward for when he comes to you the first time you call. If your dog fails to respond to the Here command three times in a single outside session, return to training the command inside for two more weeks.

The Here Command

Smithwicks... Here

- The Here command works well as an emergency command because it trains your dog to come directly and instantly to you.

1 Stand within three feet of your dog.

2 Say your dog's name once.

3 Say the command "Here" once.

4 As soon as your dog looks at you, praise him. Continue praising your dog as he comes toward you.

5 When your dog reaches you, touch his collar.

6 Give your dog a special food treat and praise him enthusiastically.

Note: You should use a treat that your dog will learn to associate only with the Here command.

7 Practice steps 1 to 6 inside your home three times each day. When your dog is coming directly and instantly to you, you can gradually move farther away from your dog.

canine good citizen test

Once your dog reliably performs the commands of basic training, the Canine Good Citizen® test presents an opportunity to further his training and build on the relationship you fostered during basic training. The Canine Good Citizen (CGC) program was developed in 1981 by the American Kennel Club (AKC), which still administers the CGC title and certificate that come with passing the 10-part test. Similar tests based on the AKC's program have been developed in countries around the world, including Canada, England and Australia.

The CGC test evaluates a dog's socialization skills, appearance, obedience and response to distractions, among other elements. The first five elements described below deal with socialization, appearance and obedience. The test also judges your abilities as a responsible dog owner and your success as your dog's trainer.

Your dog should be at least one year old before taking the CGC test and you must provide proof that he meets the vaccination requirements for the test. Your dog will be on leash during the test so make sure that you fit him securely with a collar.

Sitting for Petting

- The Canine Good Citizen Test is designed to recognize dogs who have good manners at home and in public.

- The test is made up of a series of 10 tests that the dog must pass.

1 **Accepting a Stranger**

- The evaluator approaches and then greets the owner, while ignoring the dog.

- The dog should not show signs of shyness.

2 **Sitting for Petting**

- The dog sits at his owner's side while the evaluator pets the dog on his head or body.

- The dog should not show signs of shyness.

3 **Appearance and Grooming**

- The evaluator inspects the dog and may brush him, examine his ears and pick up each front paw.

- The dog should be comfortable with the evaluator's actions.

Tip

Is there anything I must do before my dog can take the Canine Good Citizen test?

Before your dog takes the test, you must sign the Responsible Dog Owners Pledge. By signing, you agree to take care of your dog's health, safety and quality of life. You also agree to responsibly clean up after your dog and to train your dog not to be a nuisance.

What are grounds for failure? Can we retake the test if we fail?

If your dog fails any one of the 10 evaluations for the CGC test, or if he eliminates during the test, he fails. Your dog remains eligible to retake the test, so you should continue to work with him and practice the test's routines. However, if your dog exhibits aggressive behavior, such as growling or attacking a person or another dog, he fails and is barred from taking the test again.

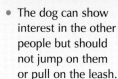

4 <u>Walk on a Loose Leash</u>

- The evaluator may use a pre-set course or use verbal instructions to direct the owner on a loose-leash walk with the dog.

- The dog should pay attention to his owner and respond to his owner's movements.

5 <u>Walk Through a Crowd</u>

- The dog and owner walk around and pass by at least three other people.

- The dog can show interest in the other people but should not jump on them or pull on the leash.

CONTINUED...

canine good citizen test *(continued)*

The last five elements of the Canine Good Citizen (CGC) test, which are described below, examine the success of your dog's training, including his ability to deal with distractions and separation from you. Successfully completing all 10 elements of the CGC test opens the door for additional training, as well as events sponsored by the American Kennel Club (AKC).

If your dog passes the CGC, you can request a high-quality certificate from the AKC, recognizing your dog as a Canine Good Citizen. Any dog, purebred or mixed breed, is eligible to take the test and earn the title

and certificate, which requires a small fee and the completion of a testing form.

To prepare for the CGC test, practice the skills and routines described below and on pages 130 to 131. You may also want to consider working with a professional dog trainer in your area for a more concentrated practice. Some trainers offer sessions specifically designed for the CGC test. Do not be discouraged if you and your dog do not pass the test. Resolve to work more diligently on problem areas and try again when you feel better prepared.

Coming When Called

6 **Sit, Down and Stay**

- The owner uses commands to have his dog sit, lie down and stay.

  Note: The dog's leash is replaced with a long line.

- The dog should stay until the evaluator tells the owner to release the dog.

7 **Coming When Called**

- The owner walks away from the dog and then calls him.

  Note: The dog's leash is replaced with a long line.

- The dog should go to the owner.

8 **Reaction to Another Dog**

- Two owners and dogs approach each other. The owners stop, shake hands and then continue walking.

- The dogs may show interest, but should not go to the other dog or owner.

Tip

How can I help my dog pass the CGC test?

If you and your dog have practiced the test's routines, you should feel well prepared for the test. There are also some other things you can do to give your dog the best chance for success. For the Appearance and Grooming test element, bathe and groom your dog as close to the testing time as possible. Before you get to the testing location, run around with your dog to get him warmed up and try to get him to eliminate before entering the test site. During the test, stay calm so that your dog will also remain calm. Also, you may praise and encourage your dog, including petting between test elements. However, you cannot offer food or toys during testing.

How do I find out about CGC tests in my area?

Ask a local dog trainer or at the local shelter about an AKC affiliate, 4-H club or qualified training organization that hosts tests in your area. The AKC Web site, www.akc.org, also has testing location information.

9 <u>Reaction to Distraction</u>

- The evaluator presents two distractions, such as dropping a chair or having a person jog by the dog.

- The dog may show slight interest or may appear slightly startled but should not run away or bark.

10 <u>Supervised Separation</u>

- The evaluator takes the dog's leash from the owner and the owner goes out of sight for three minutes.

- The dog should remember his training and manners when left with the evaluator. The dog should not bark, whine or pace while his owner is gone.

Chapter 7

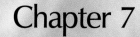

All work and no play makes Rover a dull dog. This chapter includes information on fun games you can play with your dog, such as Hide and Seek, Fetch and Tug. In addition to being a fun way to interact with your dog, most of the games in this chapter also help you and your dog practice the commands you have worked on in the previous chapters. You will also find information on creating mentally stimulating activities for your dog.

Fun Games

In this Chapter...

puppy push-ups

Puppy Push-Ups is a game that allows your dog to practice two basic commands—the Sit command (page 100) and the Down command (page 104). A Sit and a Down is considered one Puppy Push-Up.

You can play Puppy Push-Ups with your dog as a means of monitoring his progress with the Sit and Down commands. To monitor your dog's progress, count how many Puppy Push-Ups he is able to perform in a set period of time. You can use this number as a baseline for future training sessions.

With practice, your dog will improve his response time to both the Sit and Down commands.

At first, reward your dog with a treat for every correct position change. As you practice more, you can start offering a treat after two or more position changes. By offering your dog treats at different times during the game, your dog will no longer be able to predict how many commands he must complete in order to earn a treat. This is a helpful way of slowly weaning your dog off treats.

- To get your dog to perform Puppy Push-Ups, you use a lure to guide your dog into position. You will most often use a treat as a lure.

1 Kneel in front of your dog.

2 Hold a treat in your right hand close to your dog's nose.

3 Say the command "Sit."

4 Move the treat up and toward the back of your dog's head.

5 When your dog sits, give him the treat and praise him.

6 Hold a treat in your right hand close to your dog's nose.

7 Say the command "Down."

8 Lower the treat straight down toward the floor.

9 When your dog lies on the floor, give your dog the treat and praise him.

- Your dog has now completed one Puppy Push-Up.

10 Repeat steps 2 to 9 for 30 seconds, counting the number of Puppy Push-Ups your dog completes.

trading game

To play the Trading game, you trade items of various values with your dog. The Trading game teaches your dog to give up items to you when asked.

The Trading game is an excellent preventative exercise for resource guarding. Resource guarding is when a dog refuses to give up an item, such as food or a toy.

To play the Trading game, you first identify your dog's favorite items. Make sure you use a variety of items, such as food treats, balls, stuffed toys,

and squeaky toys. To encourage your dog to give up objects, you begin with his least favorite items and trade for ones he enjoys more.

The lessons learned by playing the Trading game can be helpful in everyday situations. For example, your dog may get a hold of a new item that has high reward potential, such as a piece of pizza. If your dog is comfortable with the Trading game, you should have little trouble taking this item away from him.

Give

1 Make a list of your dog's 10 favorite items, in order from least to most favorite.

Note: The items on the list should include a variety of items, such as toys, bones and food items.

2 Obtain one of your dog's least favorite items from the list.

3 Give the item to your dog and allow him to play with the item for a few seconds.

4 Place your hand on the item and say the command "Give."

5 When your dog releases the item into your hand, praise the dog and give him one of his more favorite items as a reward.

• When you start playing this game, trade a less favorite item for a more favorite item. After your dog becomes comfortable, you can start trading items on the list in different orders.

front and
center

When walking your dog, you can play the "Front and Center" game to practice his skills of walking on a loose leash, paying attention to his owner and coming when called. The "Front and Center" game is a safe and easy way to practice the Come command when there are distractions around, since your dog is on a leash during the game.

To begin playing "Front and Center" during a walk, have your dog on a loose leash at your side and then say the "Let's Go" command and begin walking forward quickly. You then say the "Come" command and jog backwards for at least five steps to have your dog practice coming to you. When your dog turns and runs toward you, you should praise him as a reward.

When playing "Front and Center" with your dog, make sure you jog backwards instead of turning around and running away from your dog. You should also make sure you do not pull your dog toward you with the leash. Your dog should turn and come to you on his own.

Let's Go

Winston... Come

- The "Front and Center" game allows your dog to practice his skills of walking on a loose leash and coming when called. You can play the "Front and Center" game randomly as you walk with your dog.

1 With your dog on a loose leash at your left side, say the command "Let's Go" and then walk forward at a quick pace.

2 Call your dog's name and say the command "Come."

3 Jog backwards at least five steps away from your dog.

4 As your dog turns and runs toward you, encourage him to keep him moving toward you.

5 When your dog is right in front of you, praise him.

how do you do

"How Do You Do" is a game that teaches your dog to sit politely in front of people instead of jumping up on them.

In order to play "How Do You Do," you will need at least one other person to help you. With your dog on a leash, approach the other person. When you reach the person, say the command "Sit" to have your dog sit politely in front of them. When your dog sits, the other person should reward your dog with a treat and then greet him by petting him on the chest.

If your dog does not sit when instructed, you should turn him away from the person for a moment and then turn back and try again. Make sure your dog does not receive a treat or praise until he sits.

While on a walk, you can ask dog-friendly strangers you meet on the street or in the park to play this game with you and your dog. Make sure you give them treats they can give to your dog as a reward before you begin playing. You should try to have your dog greet 10 new people every week by playing "How Do You Do."

- The "How Do You Do" game allows your dog to practice sitting politely in front of people instead of jumping up on them.

1 Attach your dog's leash to his collar.

2 Walk with your dog toward the other person.

3 When you arrive at the other person, say the command "Sit" to have your dog sit.

4 When your dog sits, the other person can give your dog a treat and then pet him on the chest.

Note: The other person should never reach for your dog's head, as some dogs may consider this to be threatening.

- If your dog does not sit, turn and walk away from the other person with your dog. Make sure your dog does not get a reward or praise. After 20 seconds, approach the other person again and repeat steps 3 and 4.

hide and seek

Dogs love to play games. You can make games rewarding to both you and your dog by playing games that work on his skills. "Hide and Seek" is a mentally stimulating game that lets your dog work on two skills: coming when called and keeping track of his owner.

In "Hide and Seek," you need two people: one to hold the dog's collar while the second person hides. Starting with the dog's owner as the hider helps to teach the dog to keep track of his owner. The hider takes along the dog's food bowl and hand feeds the dog his reward when he is found. These elements of the game offer two other benefits. First, holding your dog's collar gets him used to collar grabs and being touched near his collar. Second, hand feeding the reward teaches him to not nip and to grow comfortable with people around his food bowl.

"Hide and Seek" also strengthens the relationship between dog and family, especially if other family members participate. You can also teach your dog to find family members by having the person holding the dog say "Find" followed by the hider's name when releasing the dog.

1 One person, the holder, holds the dog's collar to keep him in place while the other person hides.

2 The other person, the hider, takes the dog's food bowl containing the dog's dinner and hides one room away in an obvious location, such as behind a couch.

3 The hider calls the dog's name and says "Find me."

4 The holder releases the dog.

5 As the dog searches for the hider, the hider praises the dog.

Tip

How can I make "Hide and Seek" more challenging for my dog?

Gradually hide in places where you are more difficult to find. Start the game by hiding only one room away. As your dog becomes more skilled at finding you, hide farther and farther away within the house. Eventually, you can move the game outdoors, playing in a safely enclosed area, such as a fenced yard.

Do I always have to use my dog's food and food bowl as a reward?

No. You can use the food bowl for only the first few times you play "Hide and Seek" with your dog. After your dog becomes accustomed to the game, you can then simply enthusiastically praise your dog for finding you. Using the food bowl and hand feeding your dog as a reward is useful to get your dog used to having people in and around his food bowl and helps prevent problems with resource guarding. See page 226 for more information on resource guarding. Eventually, playing the "Hide and Seek" game again is rewarding enough in itself for your dog.

Good dog

6 When the dog finds the hider, the hider praises the dog enthusiastically.

7 The hider hand feeds the dog a portion of his dinner from the dog's bowl as a reward.

• Hand feeding helps your dog to learn to avoid biting and makes the dog comfortable with people in and around his food bowl.

fetch

Fetch is a cooperative and relationship building game you can play with your dog. In this game, your dog chases a toy you throw and then brings it back and gives it to you. Fetch is commonly played with a ball.

To play Fetch, show your dog a toy and then throw it a short distance away. When your dog runs after the toy, praise him until he returns it to you. You should always end the game before your dog loses interest in the game.

Playing Fetch with your dog teaches him important lessons, such as coming back to his owner. Fetch also teaches your dog that he doesn't "own" things. This is important since it will help prevent resource guarding. For more information on resource guarding, see page 226. Playing Fetch is also a great game for the family dog to play with a child. This game teaches your dog that the child has control and it allows your child to play with your dog in a constructive manner.

- You can play Fetch with your dog to work on your dog's skills of coming back to you. Playing Fetch also teaches your dog that he does not own his toys.

- You should begin playing Fetch in a limited area inside your house, such as in a hallway with all the doors closed.

1 Show your dog the toy and then toss the toy a short distance away.

- Your dog follows the toy.

  Note: If your dog does not follow the toy, repeat step 1 using a different toy.

2 Praise your dog as he follows the toy.

Tip

Where should I begin playing Fetch with my dog?

You should start playing Fetch inside a small area of your house, such as a hallway with all the doors closed. This will prevent your dog from running away with the toy during the game. When your dog becomes more skilled at playing fetch, you can play outdoors in a safely enclosed area, such as a fenced yard.

What should I do if my dog will not return to me with the ball?

If your dog does not return to you with the ball, do not chase him. To encourage your dog to come back to you, pick up another toy and play with it yourself. Your dog will most likely be curious about what you are doing and will come to play with you.

What should I keep in mind when choosing a toy to play Fetch with?

When playing Fetch, you should make sure that the toy you choose is the right size for your dog. If the toy is too big, your dog will not be as likely to play.

Steps 4 & 5

3 When your dog picks up the toy and starts to return to you, praise him.

Note: If your dog does not pick up the toy, try tossing the toy a shorter distance.

4 When your dog returns to you, position your left hand under his mouth.

5 With your right hand, hold a treat close to your dog's nose.

6 Say the command "Give."

7 When your dog drops the toy into your left hand, give your dog the treat and praise him.

Note: As your dog becomes accustomed to the Give command, you can stop using a treat. Simply say the command "Give" to have your dog let go of the ball.

8 Repeat steps 1 to 7 three times and then put the ball away.

Note: As your dog becomes more skilled at playing Fetch, you can repeat the steps more than three times.

tug

Tug is a game that strengthens the bond between you and your dog. The object of the game is to have your dog pull on one end of a toy while you pull on the other end. The act of playing Tug provides mental and physical stimulation for your dog.

The game of Tug also allows your dog to practice self control. When playing Tug, your dog learns that he must hold still until you give the Tug command and that you determine when the game starts and stops.

In addition to learning self control, this game also provides your dog with an opportunity to practice the Give command.

You can use the game of Tug as a reward for good behavior. For example, if you call your dog away from other dogs in an off-leash park and he responds immediately, you can pull out your dog's Tug toy and reward him by playing Tug.

- You should have a special toy that is used only for playing Tug with your dog.

1 You should have your dog sit before you play a game of Tug. Say the command "Sit" to have your dog sit.

2 When your dog sits, show him the toy you use only for playing Tug.

3 Shake the toy in front of your dog to get him excited.

4 Using an excited tone of voice, say "Want to Tug?"

5 Allow your dog to take part of the toy in his mouth.

6 Tug on the toy and allow your dog to tug back.

7 Repeat step 6 for 10 seconds. Then stop tugging on the toy.

Tip

What should I keep in mind when playing Tug with my dog?

When playing Tug, you and your dog must play by the following rules:

- There is one toy and one toy only for playing Tug. When the toy is not being used for Tug, the toy should be kept out of your dog's reach.

- Your dog must sit, or perform another command you choose, before being invited to play a game of Tug.

- You (not your dog) start and stop the game.

- If your dog's teeth touch your skin at any time, the game is over for that day.

8 Hold a treat close to your dog's nose.

9 Using a calm tone of voice, say the command "Give."

10 When your dog lets go of the toy, give your dog the treat and praise him.

Note: As your dog becomes accustomed to the Give command, you can skip step **8**. Simply say "Give" to have your dog let go of the toy.

11 Repeat steps **1** to **10** once and then put the toy away.

Note: As your dog becomes more skilled at playing Tug, you can repeat the steps more than once.

recall game

The Recall game is a fun and rewarding way to teach and reinforce the Come command. The Come command could be a life-saving command for your dog. If your dog ends up in a potentially dangerous situation, you want to make sure that he will always respond to this command when you say it. The Recall game also helps your dog have a positive association with the Come command.

When you and the other participants form your circle, make sure you allow a distance between people that is appropriate for the size of your dog. If your dog has too great a distance from one person to the next, he may veer off-course and not go to each person. You should also make sure that you end the game before your dog becomes bored or tired and stops responding to the Come command.

Holding your dog's collar before giving the treat is an important element to the Recall game. You avoid playing a game of "chase," where your dog comes to you, but stays just out of reach.

1 Three or more people sit in a large circle. Everyone faces the center of the circle.

2 One person holds your dog's collar.

3 To start the game, the person releases your dog's collar.

4 Say your dog's name once and then say the command "Come."

5 As soon as your dog looks at you after you call him, praise him.

6 Continue praising your dog as he comes toward you.

Tip

What should I do if my dog is hesitant about moving from person to person?

If your dog has trouble understanding that he needs to move between people, form a very small circle to start the game. Whoever calls your dog should also open her arms wide as if inviting your dog for a hug. If your dog still resists going to the next person in the game, the person he is with should stand up, turn around and ignore your dog until he leaves.

My dog really enjoys the Recall game. Are there variations that can be helpful with other aspects of his training?

You can play the game with your family to teach your dog the names of your family members. When each person releases your dog's collar, that person should instruct your dog to go to another family member before he hears the Come command. For example, if you want your dog to go to Susie, release his collar, say "go to Susie" and point to Susie. Susie then calls your dog's name and says the command "Come."

7 When your dog reaches you, hold his collar.

8 Give your dog a treat and praise him enthusiastically.

9 Release your dog's collar.

10 Another person in the circle performs steps 4 to 9.

11 Continue moving your dog around the circle from person to person until your dog has gone to every person twice.

Note: Mix up the order that the people in the circle call your dog to keep him from anticipating where he will go next.

mentally stimulating activities

Mental stimulation is as much an important element of your dog's day-to-day regimen as eating nutritiously and exercising properly. Much of what you already do with your dog also serves to mentally stimulate him, including training basic commands, teaching him new tricks and taking him on regular walks.

Keeping your dog's brain working on constructive games and exercises prevents him from looking on his own for ways to keep his brain active. When left on his own, he may take part in mentally stimulating activities that are also destructive, such as inappropriate chewing or digging. Like physical exercise, regular mental stimulation keeps your dog happy and uses up energy that may otherwise be spent engaging in destructive behavior.

Dogs come by their curiosity naturally. If you give your dog a mentally stimulating goal to achieve or a game at which to succeed, he will be less likely to set out on his own exploration. Mental stimulation activities are also fantastic for older or injured dogs whose physical abilities are limited.

Kong™ Hunt

1 Stuff a Kong™ with food treats. For information on stuffing a Kong™, see page 234.

2 Show your dog the Kong™ and then hide it where your dog will be able to find it easily, such as behind furniture.

3 Take your dog away from the location where the Kong™ is hidden.

4 Work with your dog on simple commands, such as Sit (see page 100) and Down (see page 104), for one minute.

5 After one minute, allow your dog to look for the hidden Kong™.

Note: If your dog seems unsure about what you want him to do, help him find the Kong™.

6 Praise your dog when he finds the Kong™ and allow him to eat the treats inside.

Note: You can gradually hide the Kong™ in more difficult locations.

Tip

Where should I start when considering mentally stimulating activities for my dog?

Find out what kind of activity your dog's breed was bred for and then start him out with a related activity that he may take to naturally. For example, if your dog is a retriever, encourage him to retrieve things when you play. If your dog was bred to hunt or track, have him use those skills to find his dinner.

Are there any mentally stimulating activities that my dog can perform while I am away at work?

If your dog is left alone when you go to work, you can use the Kong™ Hunt game to keep him occupied while you are away. Instead of feeding him breakfast from his food bowl, stuff three Kongs™ and hide them around your house before you leave for the day. Your dog can then spend his alone time hunting for his meal while you are away.

Shell Game

Tracking

1 Place three plastic containers upside down on the floor.

2 Show your dog a biscuit and then place it under one of the containers.

3 Move the containers around and mix them up.

4 Allow your dog to sniff at the containers and try to determine which container the biscuit is under.

5 When your dog locates the biscuit, praise him and allow him to uncover and eat the biscuit.

1 Divide half of your dog's meal into several small portions.

2 Place small piles of food around your house or yard to create a trail of food that your dog will follow.

3 At the end of the trail, partially hide your dog's food bowl containing the rest of his meal.

4 Take your dog to the beginning of the trail. Then allow him to follow the trail and find his food bowl.

Chapter 8

This chapter includes a wide variety of tricks that you can teach your dog and use to impress and amaze your family and friends. Read this chapter to learn how to teach your dog to perform tricks, such as Take a Bow, Wave, Dance, Roll Over, and of course, Shake a Paw.

Cool Tricks

In this Chapter...

read

If you are just beginning to teach your dog some tricks, the Read trick is a good one to start with. This trick is easy to teach. In fact, you may consider having your child teach this trick. Training the Read trick builds your dog's confidence for learning other tricks and your child will love teaching it.

All you need to teach the Read trick is a large piece of paper to make a sign, a treat and the ability to get your dog to wag his tail. Most dogs wag their tails with very little encouragement, often just with a little sweet talk. When you sweet talk your dog, you say something positive in a pleasant tone so that he wags his tail.

While sweet talking, hold a sign in front of him that says "Wag your tail." Your dog will look as if he is reading the sign and start wagging his tail. If you know what words and tone will make your dog wag his tail gently or quickly, you can use those words and tone and create another sign that reads "Wag your tail gently" or "Wag your tail quickly."

1 Make a sign that reads "Wag your tail."

2 With your dog standing, hold the sign you made in front of him.

3 Talk to your dog in an engaging, pleasant voice to get him to wag his tail.

• Your dog wags his tail.

4 When your dog wags his tail, praise your dog and give him a treat.

Note: If your dog does not wag his tail, you can play a game with him, such as Fetch (page 142) or Tug (page 144), to get him in the mood to wag his tail. Then repeat steps 2 to 4.

cookie on paw

The "Cookie On Paw" trick is an excellent confidence building activity for you and your dog. This trick is well-suited to early training since it is a simple way to practice basic commands.

You can teach the "Cookie On Paw" trick to help practice the Off command (page 112) and exercise your dog's self-control. In this trick, you place a cookie treat on your dog's paw while he is in the Down position (page 104). The purpose of this trick is to have your dog resist the temptation to eat the cookie until you give him permission. If your dog

has sensitive paws, you can place the cookie on the floor in front of his paws when teaching this trick.

When you first start training the "Cookie On Paw" trick, your dog may stare at the cookie while waiting for permission to eat it. As your dog becomes better at performing this trick, you can practice having your dog look at you instead of staring at the cookie. Once your dog has mastered the "Cookie On Paw" trick, you can use this trick to demonstrate how well-behaved your dog is.

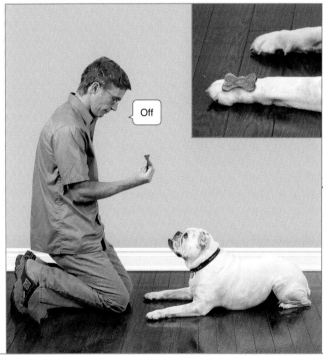

1 Start with your dog in the Down position. For information on the Down position, see page 104.

2 Kneel in front of your dog.

3 Show your dog a cookie and say the command "Off." For information on the Off command, see page 112.

4 Place the cookie on one of your dog's front paws.

5 Praise your dog while he stays off the cookie.

Note: If your dog attempts to eat the cookie, temporarily cover the cookie with your hand.

6 After five seconds, remove the cookie from your dog's paw and give the cookie to your dog, saying "Take It."

• You can gradually increase the length of time your dog must stay off the cookie before getting the cookie.

catch

After teaching your dog the Catch trick, you can play catch with him, tossing a favorite toy or a tennis ball to him so that he catches it in mid-air. To start training, however, use a light treat that is easy to toss, floats gently and is easy for your dog to catch in mid-air. A good treat to try is a puffed-cheese snack.

If your dog fails to catch the treat when you begin training, make sure that you get to the fallen treat before your dog does. You want your dog to learn that the only way he can taste that treat is to catch it in mid-air. Until your dog becomes adept at catching treats, you may find it useful to have a helper on hand to snatch any dropped treats away from your dog.

When your dog starts to reliably catch treats you drop from directly over his head, you can gradually move away from your dog and toss the treats toward his mouth. You can also introduce a toy or ball into the training routine for him to catch.

Catch

1 Start with your dog in the Sit position (page 100).

2 Stand in front of your dog, making sure you are close to your dog.

3 Hold a light treat, such as a puffed-cheese snack, in your right hand.

4 Position your right hand about 6 inches above your dog's head.

• Your dog tilts his head back to look up at the treat.

5 Say the command "Catch."

6 Drop the treat directly over your dog's mouth.

• Your dog opens his mouth and catches the treat.

7 When your dog catches the treat, praise your dog.

• If your dog does not catch the treat and the treat falls to the floor, quickly cover the treat with your foot. Do not allow your dog to eat the treat. Then repeat steps 3 to 7.

back up

Some dogs may find it difficult to move away from their owner. Learning the "Back Up" trick helps to reassure your dog that being separated from you is not necessarily a bad thing. In fact, successfully performing the "Back Up" trick can even boost your dog's confidence.

When you begin training, you want your dog to move away from you, or back up, in a fairly straight direction. You also want to make sure that he cannot turn around and walk away instead of backing up.

Set up the training in as narrow an area as you can find that is still comfortable for your dog. For example, train the "Back Up" trick in a narrow hallway or alongside a bed that is positioned close to a wall.

The "Back Up" trick is not a very difficult one for your dog to learn. You can start out slowly, rewarding your dog for backing up only a step or two. If your dog is hesitant to back up when you begin the training, try prodding him along by nudging his front toes with your foot.

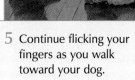

1 Start with your dog in the Stand position (page 102).

2 Stand in front of your dog.

3 Say the command "Back Up."

4 With your hands just below your waist level and the backs of your hands facing your dog, flick your fingers at your dog. This is the hand signal for "Back Up."

5 Continue flicking your fingers as you walk toward your dog.

• Your dog backs up.

6 When your dog backs up two steps, give your dog a treat and praise him.

• If your dog does not back up, you can gently nudge your dog's toes with your foot.

Note: As your dog becomes comfortable, you can gradually increase the number of steps he takes.

hugs

Teaching your dog to hug is the kind of feel-good trick that most people enjoy. It is an especially useful trick when family members welcome their dog jumping up on them because this trick will teach your dog to jump up on you only when asked.

Hugs is a fantastic trick to teach your dog if he is inclined to jump up on people. However, you must first train your dog to sit when greeting people so that he knows it is never acceptable to randomly jump up on people. For information on training your dog to sit when greeting people, see page 100.

With the Hugs command or hand signal, you teach your dog to know when it is acceptable to jump up on people, which is by invitation only. The Hugs trick helps to minimize the unwelcome behavior of jumping up uninvited because you reward with praise only after he jumps up when invited. You ignore him when he jumps up uninvited.

Reserve your dog's food rewards in this training for sitting after the hug. Rewarding him with food after he sits helps keep his jumping-up behavior under control.

1 Start with your dog in the Sit position (page 100).

2 Stand in front of your dog, making sure you are standing close to your dog.

3 Say the command "Hugs."

4 Depending on the size of your dog, pat your chest or your knees with both hands in an excited manner. This is the hand signal for Hugs.

• Your dog jumps up and places his front paws on you.

5 Praise your dog and pet him on his sides.

My dog will not jump up on me no matter how hard I pat my chest or knees. What should I do?

If you have previously encouraged your dog to not jump up on people, then getting him to respond to this training may take a little coaxing. While practicing the steps below, you can try talking very excitedly in step 3 and holding a toy in your right hand in step 4. Remember not to use a food reward, though, as you will need that for training your dog to sit after the hug.

How do I train my dog to not jump up on people?

If your dog is prone to jumping up on people uninvited, training the Hugs trick may help control this behavior. When you train your dog to perform a behavior on cue and then ask for that behavior only in certain circumstances, the unwanted behavior seems to decline. Also, if your dog really enjoys jumping up on people, you can use the behavior itself as a reward. You can have your dog perform some commands and then use the Hug trick as a reward.

6 When you want to end the hug, step back from your dog until you are out of your dog's reach.

• Your dog's front paws return to the floor.

• Once the hug is over, use the Sit command to have your dog sit. Having your dog sit after a hug and rewarding the sit with a food treat teaches your dog that, although jumping up is nice, sitting politely will earn him a treat.

7 To have your dog sit, say the command "Sit."

8 When your dog is sitting, give your dog a treat and praise him.

speak

You teach your dog the Speak command so that he will bark, or speak, when you ask him to. The command is joined by a hand signal that mimics a speaking gesture, that is, your right hand opening and closing as a mouth would open and close.

Before beginning to train this command, you need to know what reliably makes your dog bark. For most dogs, the noise of the doorbell does the trick. You will need a helper to ring the doorbell so that you can stay with your dog while training this command.

When training the Speak command, you verbally praise your dog after he speaks. When you want him to be quiet, you give your dog the Shush command and give him a food treat when he becomes quiet. This teaches your dog that while speaking on cue is good because he receives praise, becoming quiet afterwards is even better because he receives a food treat. You should never offer your dog a food treat as a reward for speaking, as this could potentially create a barking problem.

1 Start with your dog in the Stand position (page 102).

2 Stand in front of your dog.

3 Say the command "Speak" in an excited manner.

4 Position your right hand 6 inches from your dog's nose. With your fingers on top and your thumb on the bottom, open and close your hand. This is the hand signal for Speak.

5 Immediately have the other person ring the doorbell.

• Your dog barks.

6 Allow your dog to bark a few times and praise your dog.

Note: Once your dog associates the Speak command and the hand signal with barking, you no longer need another person to ring the doorbell.

Tip

My dog tends to bark a lot. Should I still teach him the Speak command?

If your dog barks excessively, the Speak command may help you control his behavior. When you train your dog to practice a behavior on cue and then ask for that behavior only in certain circumstances, the unwanted behavior is likely to decline. For information on excessive barking, see page 212. After you have trained the Speak command, you can also use the command as a reward. Have your dog perform some commands and then have him speak as his reward.

My dog does not always bark for the doorbell. Are there other tools that I can try?

Observe your dog's behavior to find out whether something else in or around your house encourages him to bark. Then you can use your helper to manage whatever it is that makes your dog bark while you go through the steps below. You can also try waving one of your dog's favorite toys around in front of him to get him excited enough to bark. You can also try barking at your dog to get him to "answer" back.

7 To quiet your dog after he speaks, place a food treat in your right hand and close your hand into a fist.

8 Say the command "Shush."

9 With your fingers facing your dog, place your right hand close to your dog's nose and allow him to sniff your hand.

- Since your dog cannot sniff and bark at the same time, your dog is quiet.

10 After your dog has been quiet for approximately five seconds, give him the food treat and praise him.

Note: Once your dog associates the Shush command with being quiet, you can use the command without the treat to have your dog stop barking.

take a bow

The "Take a Bow" trick is similar to other tricks in that it allows you to work closely with your dog on something that is enjoyable. When your dog takes a bow, his elbows bend, his chest is close to the floor and his hind quarters are in the air.

Most dogs are able to learn the "Take a Bow" trick quickly. However, to help your dog more easily grasp this trick, make sure that you say the entire command, "Take a Bow," while training him.

If you say "Bow" only, your dog may think that you are saying "Down."

If your dog has difficulty with this trick, try rewarding him for small successes. For example, give him a treat as soon as he starts to bend his elbows. Gradually progress, rewarding for other small milestones, until your dog can assume the "Take a Bow" position.

Training with a Lure

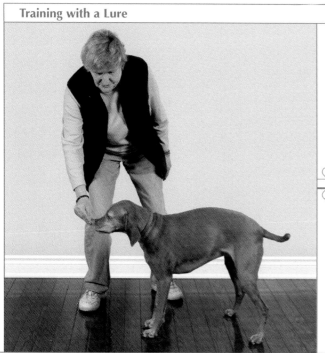

Take a Bow

- When you first start training your dog to take a bow, you use a lure to guide your dog into position. You will most often use a treat as a lure.

1 Start with your dog in the Stand position (page 102).

2 Stand to the right of your dog, facing your dog's right side.

3 Hold a treat between the fingertips and thumb of your right hand, with your palm facing your dog.

4 Say the command "Take a Bow."

5 Quickly lower the treat past your dog's nose to the floor between his front paws.

- As your dog quickly lowers his head to follow the treat, his elbows bend and his chest is close to the floor. Your dog's hind quarters remain in the air.

6 Give your dog the treat immediately and praise him.

Tip

My dog goes into the Down position instead of the "Take a Bow" position. What can I do?

When first training the "Take a Bow" trick, your dog may get confused because of the similarity of the "Take a Bow" trick and the Down command. The training routines with a lure for both positions require you to lower a treat to the floor. To help your dog learn the "Take a Bow" trick, you can place your left hand underneath your dog, in front of his back legs, without touching him, to prevent him from dropping into the Down position.

Training after the Lure

Take a Bow

- After your dog responds reliably when lured with a treat, you can stop using the treat to guide your dog into position. You use a treat only as a reward after your dog performs the trick.

1 Perform steps 1 and 2 on page 160.

2 Say the command "Take a Bow."

3 With your right palm facing your dog, sweep your right hand toward your dog. This is the hand signal for "Take a Bow."

- Your dog takes a bow, with his elbows bent, his chest close to the floor and his hind quarters in the air.

4 Give your dog a special food treat and praise him.

Note: If your dog does not take a bow, turn away from him for five seconds and then repeat steps 1 to 4. After three unsuccessful attempts, return to training the "Take a Bow" trick with a treat lure.

shake a paw

Training your dog to perform the "Shake a Paw" trick is rewarding for both you and your dog. Grasping your dog's paw in this gentle manner will strengthen the bond between you and your dog, especially when the grasp is followed by a tasty treat.

This is a trick that your dog can perform with other people. For people who are afraid of dogs, this trick is a good way to introduce them to your dog. People often see shaking a dog's paw as a familiar and friendly greeting.

The "Shake a Paw" trick is one that most dogs are able to learn fairly quickly. You practice the trick by using the "Shake a Paw" command, accompanied by a hand signal and a favorite treat. The hand signal is simply cupping your right hand with your right palm facing up. With practice and encouragement, your dog will quickly become comfortable with this trick. Eventually, you will only need to use the command or the hand signal to have your dog perform this trick.

Training with a Lure

Shake a Paw

- When you first start training your dog to shake a paw, you use a lure to guide your dog into position. You will most often use a treat as a lure.

1 Start with your dog in the Sit position (page 100).

2 Place a treat in your left hand and close your hand into a fist.

3 Place your left hand close to your dog's nose.

4 Say the command "Shake a Paw."

5 Move your closed left hand to the left.

- As your dog moves his head and shoulders to follow the treat, his paw will lift off the floor.

6 With your right hand, palm facing up and slightly cupped, catch your dog's paw.

7 Shake your dog's paw as you give your dog the treat in your left hand and praise him.

Is there another trick I can teach my dog after he learns how to shake a paw?

Once your dog knows how to shake a paw, you can easily teach him how to give you a high five. To train for the "High Five" trick, position your cupped right hand in front of your dog at his chest level. As your dog reaches to give you his paw, quickly turn your hand so that your open palm is facing your dog and your fingers are pointing up. Then say the command "High Five" and tap his paw. Give him a treat and praise.

Training after the Lure

Shake a Paw

- After your dog responds reliably when lured with a treat, you can stop using the treat to guide your dog into position. You use a treat only as a reward after your dog performs the trick.

1 Start with your dog in the Sit position.

2 Say the command "Shake a Paw."

3 Extend your cupped right hand toward your dog, with your palm facing up. This is the hand signal for "Shake a Paw."

- Your dog raises his paw toward your cupped right hand.

4 When your dog raises his paw, catch and shake his paw.

5 Give your dog a special food treat and praise him.

Note: If your dog does not raise his paw, turn away from your dog for five seconds and then repeat steps 1 to 5. After three unsuccessful attempts, return to training the "Shake a Paw" trick with a treat lure.

wave

Teaching your dog to perform a trick, such as the Wave trick, can help strengthen your relationship with your dog. Before you can teach your dog how to wave, you must first teach your dog how to shake a paw. You use the hand signal from the "Shake a Paw" trick to teach your dog the Wave trick. For information on the "Shake a Paw" trick, see page 162.

The Wave trick is one that you can try early on in your dog's training, which can help to build your confidence in your ability to train your dog.

To teach the Wave trick, you start by standing in front of your dog with your right hand cupped and your palm facing up. Because your dog thinks he is to perform the "Shake a Paw" trick, he will reach out to place his paw in your hand. You then move your hand to prevent him from shaking a paw, which will encourage him to move his paw up and down in a waving motion. At the same time, you say the command "Wave."

Training with a Lure

- When you first start training your dog to wave, you use your cupped right hand as a lure to guide your dog into position.

1 Start with your dog in the Sit position (page 100).

2 Stand in front of your dog.

3 Bend over and extend your cupped right hand toward your dog's chest level, with your palm facing up.

4 When your dog raises his paw toward your cupped right hand, say the command "Wave" and move your hand from side to side so your dog cannot touch it.

- Your dog moves his paw up and down, trying to touch your right hand.

5 Give your dog a treat and praise him.

Will my dog wave even from a long distance?

After your dog can reliably perform this trick, you can use either the Wave command or the hand signal from across a room and your dog should perform a wave. Before too long, you may be able to wave goodbye when you leave for work and your dog will wave back.

Training after the Lure

Wave

- After your dog responds reliably when lured by your cupped hand, you can stop using your hand to guide your dog.

1 Perform steps 1 and 2 on page 164.

2 Say the command "Wave."

3 With your right hand at your waist level and your palm facing your dog, wave your hand from side to side. This is the hand signal for Wave.

- Your dog waves by moving his paw up and down in the air.

4 When your dog waves, give your dog a special food treat and praise him.

Note: If your dog does not wave, turn away from your dog for five seconds and then repeat steps 1 to 4. After three unsuccessful attempts, return to training the Wave trick using your cupped right hand as a lure.

sit pretty

The "Sit Pretty" trick is a fun way for you and your dog to show off as most people find this to be a charming trick. When you use the "Sit Pretty" command or hand signal, your dog goes into a position where he balances on his hind quarters with his front paws in the air. The position of your dog's front paws can be curled into his chest, crossed or sticking out.

You should start practicing this command in the corner of a room. Training the "Sit Pretty" trick in a corner allows your dog to lean against the walls in the corner to help him balance. You should be relatively close to your dog, practically toe to toe, which will also help your dog feel comfortable with the trick. With practice, your dog will be able to move away from the corner when performing the "Sit Pretty" trick.

After your dog can reliably perform this trick, you may work with him to gradually build up the amount of time he holds the "Sit Pretty" position.

Training with a Lure

Sit Pretty

- When you start training your dog to sit pretty, you use a lure to guide your dog into position. You will most often use a treat as a lure.

1 Start with your dog in the Sit position (page 100) in a corner of a room.

2 Stand in front of your dog.

3 Hold a treat between the fingertips and thumb of your right hand, with your palm facing down.

4 Hold the treat close to your dog's nose.

5 Say the command "Sit Pretty."

6 Move the treat up and back toward your dog's forehead, keeping the treat slightly out of his reach.

- As your dog lifts up his head and shoulders to follow the treat, his front paws rise off the floor and he balances on his hind quarters.

7 Give your dog the treat immediately and praise him.

Tip

Is this trick appropriate for all dogs?

No. The "Sit Pretty" trick is usually more difficult for long-bodied dogs, such as Basset Hounds, and for deep-chested dogs, such as Doberman Pinschers. In addition, if your dog has back or hip difficulty, you should not practice this trick with him. Other dogs may also find it too challenging to perform the "Sit Pretty" trick because of other physical ailments.

My dog starts to follow the lure but then he stops. What can I do?

When you hold the treat between your thumb and index finger, try wiggling your other fingers so that the extra motion entices your dog to follow the lure all the way up. Also, you can reward for even small successes. For example, when your dog's paws leave the floor, give him a treat. Then you can gradually progress, giving treats for other small milestones, until he can attain the "Sit Pretty" position.

Training after the Lure

- After your dog responds reliably when lured with a treat, you can stop using the treat to guide your dog into position. You use a treat only as a reward after your dog performs the trick.

1 Perform steps **1** and **2** on page 166.

2 Say the command "Sit Pretty."

3 With the fingertips and thumb of your right hand together, move your hand, palm down, until it is 6 inches above your dog's head. This is the hand signal for "Sit Pretty."

- Your dog raises his front paws and balances on his hind quarters.

4 Give your dog a special food treat and praise him.

Note: If your dog does not raise his front paws and balance on his hind quarters, turn away from your dog for five seconds and then repeat steps **1** to **4**. After three unsuccessful attempts, return to training the "Sit Pretty" trick with a treat lure.

dance

The Dance trick builds upon the skills learned in the "Sit Pretty" trick as you train your dog to stand up out of the "Sit Pretty" position and stay on his hind legs for several seconds. Before you begin training the Dance trick, make sure that your dog can reliably perform the "Sit Pretty" trick. For information on the "Sit Pretty" trick, see page 166.

The Dance trick is one that some dogs have trouble performing, though smaller dogs tend to take to the trick more easily than larger dogs. The Dance trick is usually more difficult for long-bodied dogs, such as Basset Hounds, and for deep-chested dogs, such as Doberman Pinschers. In addition, if your dog has back or hip difficulty, you should not teach this trick to him.

Do not be surprised if it takes some time before your dog can dance for more than a few seconds. With practice, he will gradually build up his time in the Dance position.

Training with a Lure

Dance

- When you first start training your dog to dance, you use a lure to guide your dog into position. You will most often use a treat as a lure.

1 Start with your dog in the Sit Pretty position (page 166).

2 Stand in front of your dog.

3 With your palm facing down, hold a treat between the fingertips and thumb of your right hand.

4 Hold the treat about six inches above your dog's head.

5 Say the command "Dance."

6 Slowly move the treat straight up, keeping the treat slightly out of your dog's reach.

- Your dog stands on his hind legs to reach the treat. Your dog may jump up and down.

7 Give your dog the treat immediately and praise him.

Tip

My dog cannot hold the Dance position very long. How can I help him increase his time?

As with any trick that your dog has early difficulty with, reward for even the smallest successes. For example, when training with a lure, drop the lure down periodically to offer your dog a tiny piece of the treat and then bring the lure back up again. When training with the hand signal, try to drop your wiggling fingers down periodically to keep your dog interested.

Can I get my dog to take steps or make other movements while in the Dance position?

Once your dog responds reliably when lured with a treat and can hold the Dance position for several seconds, you can encourage him to walk forward a few steps while on his hind legs.

In the steps on page 168, after you move the treat up in step 6, slowly move the treat toward you, keeping the treat up. Your dog should remain standing on his hind legs and then walk or jump forward to reach the treat. When training after the lure, move your wiggling fingers toward you to encourage your dog to walk or jump forward.

Training after the Lure

Dance

- After your dog responds reliably when lured with a treat, you can stop using the treat to guide your dog. You use a treat only as a reward after your dog performs the trick.

1 Start with your dog in the Sit Pretty position.

2 Stand in front of your dog.

3 Say the command "Dance."

4 Wiggle the fingers of your right hand 12 inches above your dog's head. This is the hand signal for Dance.

- Your dog dances while standing on his hind legs. Your dog may jump up and down.

5 When your dog dances, give your dog a special food treat and praise him.

Note: If your dog does not dance, turn away from your dog for five seconds and then repeat steps 1 to 5. After three unsuccessful attempts, you should return to training the Dance trick with a treat lure.

spin

In the Spin trick, your dog spins around in a fairly small circle in the counter-clockwise direction. This trick is fun for both you and your dog and most dogs find the Spin trick an easy one to learn.

All you need to begin training the Spin trick is a treat to lure your dog. Starting with the treat in front of your dog's nose, you move your hand in a counter-clockwise circle toward his tail. You want him to follow your hand, starting the small circle that leads

to the full spin. After he has completed the spin and is again facing you, you can reward with the treat.

Even though this is a fairly simple trick, your dog may have trouble completing a full spin when you first start training. If your dog gets off to a slow start with this trick, remember to reward for even the smallest successes. With time and practice, he will be able to spin all the way around.

Training with a Lure

Spin

- When you first start training your dog to spin, you use a lure to guide your dog. You will most often use a treat as a lure.

1 Start with your dog in the Stand position (page 102).

2 Stand in front of your dog.

3 Hold a treat between the index finger and thumb of your right hand. Your other fingers are curled in and your palm is facing down.

4 Hold the treat close to your dog's nose.

5 Say the command "Spin."

6 Using a circular motion, slowly move the treat counter-clockwise toward your dog's hind quarters and then back toward you.

- As your dog follows the treat, he walks in a circle.

7 Give your dog the treat immediately and praise him.

Tip

Can I have my dog spin in a clockwise circle?

Yes, but you want him to associate the command "Spin" with going in a counter-clockwise direction. Instead, use the "Turn" command to teach him to go in a clockwise direction. When training with a lure using the steps below, change the command name in step 5 to "Turn." Then in step 6 below, lure your dog in a clockwise direction. When following the steps below to train after the lure, change the command name in step 2 to "Turn." In step 3, move your index finger in a clockwise direction. When your dog completes the turn, praise him.

Can I combine the Spin trick with other tricks in my dog's training?

The Spin trick is a fun one to combine with the Dance trick, after your dog has mastered holding the Dance position for several seconds. Use the Spin hand signal to get your dog to spin while he is in the Dance position. For information on the Dance trick, see page 168.

Training after the Lure

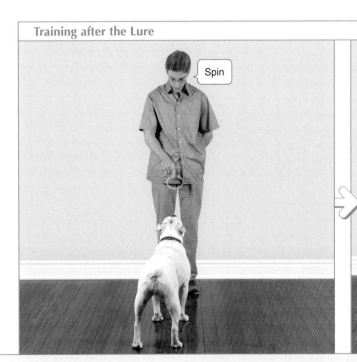

- After your dog responds reliably when lured with a treat, you can stop using the treat to guide your dog. You use a treat only as a reward after your dog performs the trick.

1 Perform steps 1 and 2 on page 170.

2 Say the command "Spin."

3 With your index finger pointing down, your other fingers curled in and your palm facing down, move your index finger in a counter-clockwise circle. This is the hand signal for Spin.

- Your dog spins by walking in a tight circle.

4 When your dog spins, give your dog a special food treat and praise him.

Note: If your dog does not spin, turn away from your dog for five seconds and then repeat steps 1 to 4. After three unsuccessful attempts, you should return to training the Spin trick with a treat lure.

play possum

Teaching your dog to perform tricks is an activity that is fun and relationship building. Performing tricks also allows you and your dog to show off. The "Play Possum" trick is one favorite.

"Play Possum" is an intermediate-level trick that is both fun to watch and useful if your dog is around people who are afraid of dogs. Seeing your dog in the "Play Possum" position may help reduce their fear of your dog.

Your dog is in the "Play Possum" position when he is lying down on his side with his head resting on the floor. You work with your dog to get to this position by using the "Play Possum" command and a hand signal. The hand signal involves pointing with the index finger of your right hand while your other fingers are curled in and your thumb is flat. Also, when you start training the "Play Possum" trick, you will need to use a lure, such as one of your dog's favorite treats, to guide your dog into position.

Training with a Lure

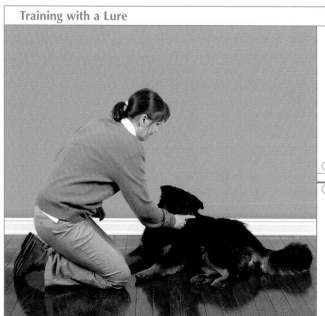

Play Possum

- When you first start training your dog to play possum, you use a lure to guide your dog into position. You will most often use a treat as a lure.

1 Start with your dog in the Settle position (page 106).

2 Kneel in front of your dog.

3 Hold a treat between the thumb, pinky, ring and middle finger of your right hand.

4 Hold the treat close to your dog's nose, with your index finger pointing toward his ear.

5 Say the command "Play Possum."

6 Bring the treat along your dog's body toward the hip that is up. Keep the treat close to your dog at all times.

- As your dog twists his head and shoulders to reach the treat, he will lie down on his side.

7 Bring the treat back toward your dog's nose and then lower the treat to the floor.

8 When your dog's head is on the floor, give him the treat immediately and praise him.

Tip

From what other positions can my dog and I perform the "Play Possum" trick?

If you are in a situation where kneeling is inappropriate or uncomfortable, such as when greeting guests who are afraid of dogs, you can train your dog to respond to the "Play Possum" command while you are standing. As with kneeling beside your dog, use the command or hand signal to have your dog play possum. With practice, you can also have your dog play possum from positions other than Settle, such as by using the Sit command or the Stand command.

Training after the Lure

Play Possum

- After your dog responds reliably when lured with a treat, you can stop using the treat to guide your dog into position. You use a treat only as a reward after your dog performs the trick.

1 Perform steps 1 and 2 on page 172.

2 Say the command "Play Possum."

3 Point the index finger of your right hand at your dog. Your other fingers are curled in and your thumb is flat. This is the hand signal for "Play Possum."

- Your dog plays possum.

4 When your dog plays possum, give your dog a special food treat and praise him.

Note: If your dog does not play possum, turn away from your dog for five seconds and then repeat steps 1 to 4. After three unsuccessful attempts, return to training the "Play Possum" trick with a treat lure.

roll over

The "Roll Over" command is a valuable trick you can use to reinforce the trusting relationship between you and your dog. This exercise involves your dog rolling over from one side to the other, exposing his abdomen in between. A dog will usually not expose his abdomen unless he is comfortable in his environment and he trusts his owner. It is not uncommon for a dog to roll over at home with ease, but encounter problems in a class situation.

To begin the roll over trick, your dog starts in the Settle position. For information on the Settle position, see page 106. To make your dog's roll easier, you should consider the position of his hind legs to determine which direction is easier for him to roll. For example, if your dog's hind legs are out to the left, he will more easily roll to the right.

If your dog is assertive, he may not want to expose his abdomen, so it is important for you to be patient. You can practice the "Roll Over" command repeatedly, alternating this command with the Sit, Down and Stand commands.

If your dog is prone to bloat or has problems with his spine or joints, then you should avoid this trick.

Training with a Lure

Roll over

Step 7

- • When you start training your dog to roll over on command, you use a lure to guide your dog. You will most often use a treat as a lure.

1 Start with your dog in the Settle position (page 106).

2 Kneel beside your dog and hold a treat in your right hand, close to his nose.

3 In a circular movement, bring the treat along your dog's body toward the hip that is up.

4 As your dog turns his head to follow the treat, say the command "Roll Over."

5 Continuing the circular movement, bring the treat up around your dog's head, keeping the treat close to your dog at all times.

6 As your dog twists his head and shoulders to reach the treat, tickle his abdomen.

7 When your dog rolls over onto his other side, give your dog the treat immediately and praise him.

Tip

I am having difficulty getting my dog to roll over. What can I do?

If your dog is having trouble with the "Roll Over" command or does not want to expose his abdomen, try breaking the trick down into smaller steps that you can reward individually. For example, if your dog turns his head to look at the treat over his shoulder, give him a reward for that success and then build up step by step.

Why does my dog only roll to one side?

You may notice that your dog prefers to lie on a particular side in the Settle position. Dogs are left or right sided, the same way people are left or right handed and this makes lying on one side more comfortable. Train your dog to roll over in the direction that is most comfortable first. When he is proficient, you can train him to roll over in the opposite direction.

Training after the Lure

Roll over

- After your dog responds reliably to the "Roll Over" command, you can stop using the treat to guide your dog. You use a treat only as a reward after your dog rolls over.

1 Kneel beside your dog.

2 Say the command "Roll Over."

3 With your right hand flat, your palm facing in, rotate your wrist to make a circle with your hand in the direction you want the dog to roll. This is the hand signal for "Roll Over."

- Your dog rolls over.

4 When your dog rolls over, give your dog a special food treat and praise him.

Note: If your dog does not roll over, turn away from your dog for five seconds and then repeat steps **1** to **4**. After three unsuccessful attempts, return to training the "Roll Over" command with a treat lure.

crawl

When your dog performs the Crawl trick, he has his abdomen near the ground and crawls forward by pulling with his front legs and pushing with his hind legs. The Crawl trick is often performed in conjunction with the "Roll Over" and "Play Possum" tricks.

Crawl is a challenging trick to learn. Your dog may have difficulty with slippery floors or he may try to raise himself off the floor instead of crawling as he tries to figure out what you want. To encourage your dog during this training, make sure you offer him a

tempting treat and be ready to reward with that treat for even the smallest forward movement.

During early training, you kneel down next to your dog so that you can use one hand to manipulate the treat and teach the hand signal, while keeping the other hand lightly on your dog's back so that he stays down when following the treat. The hand signal for the Crawl trick simulates the scratching that you do on the ground while training with a lure. Eventually, you will be able to give the hand signal while you are standing to have your dog Crawl.

Training with a Lure

- When you first start training your dog to crawl, you use a lure to guide your dog. You will most often use a treat as a lure.

1 Start with your dog in the Down position (see page 104).

2 Kneel beside your dog and place your left hand gently on his back to prevent him from standing.

3 Holding a treat between the fingertips and thumb of your right hand, place your hand on the floor between your dog's paws.

4 Say the command "Crawl."

5 Slowly drag the lure along the floor, scratching the floor with your fingertips and thumb.

- Your dog crawls forward a few inches to follow the treat.

6 Give your dog the treat immediately and praise him.

Tip

My dog insists on standing up even though I have my hand on his back. What can I do?

If your dog tries to stand up to follow the lure, practice the Crawl trick under a low object, such as a coffee table or raised knee. Remember to keep the treat low to the floor so that he can reach it without getting up. You may also want to check the floor surface that you are training on. Some dogs do not like to crawl on hard surfaces. Try practicing on a softer surface, such as carpet or a rug, or even outdoors on grass.

Training after the Lure

Crawl

- After your dog responds reliably when lured with a treat, you can stop using the treat to guide your dog. You use a treat only as a reward after your dog performs the trick.

1 Start with your dog in the Down position.

2 Stand in front of your dog.

3 Say the command "Crawl."

4 With your right hand at waist level and your palm facing down, make a scratching motion. This is the hand signal for Crawl.

- With his abdomen close to the floor, your dog crawls forward.

5 When your dog crawls forward two steps, give your dog a special food treat and praise him.

Note: If your dog does not crawl, turn away from your dog for five seconds and then repeat steps 1 to 5. After three unsuccessful attempts, return to training the Crawl trick with a treat lure.

over

You can train your dog to jump over obstacles by using the Over command. This is a fun trick to teach and it offers an additional form of exercise for your dog that you can practice while walking in the park or hiking. Teaching the Over trick is useful if you plan to pursue more advanced training with your dog, such as agility training or competitive obedience.

Before you begin training for this trick, check with your veterinarian to make sure your dog is ready to try jumping over obstacles. Your dog should be well over a year old, as young dogs can injure themselves when directed to jump too early.

When training your dog to jump over obstacles, make sure you work in a safe environment, such as a fenced yard. You should also start off with low hurdles that your dog will be able to jump over easily. For obstacles, you can try two small piles of bricks with a broom stick across them, a small pile of logs or a hula hoop that you hold close to the ground.

Training with a Lure

Over

- When you first start training your dog to jump over an obstacle, you use a leash and a lure to guide your dog over the obstacle. You will most often use a treat as a lure.

1 Attach the leash to your dog's collar.

2 Walk with your dog to the obstacle.

3 Say the command "Over."

4 With your right hand, toss a treat over the obstacle.

5 As your dog jumps over the obstacle, you walk alongside the obstacle holding the leash.

Note: When first training the Over trick, your dog may walk over the obstacle.

6 When your dog goes over the obstacle, praise him.

- Your dog eats the treat on the other side of the obstacle.

Tip

How high can I place the obstacles for my dog to try to jump over?

The best way to estimate how high your dog can jump is to first measure his height at his shoulder. Most dogs can comfortably jump about as high as their height at the shoulder. For example, if he is between 10 and 14 inches tall at the shoulder, he should be able to jump over a height of 12 inches comfortably. If he is between 18 and 22 inches at the shoulder, his jump height should be around 20 inches.

What are some other ways that my dog and I can practice this trick?

Another fun way to practice the Over trick is to train your dog to do wider jumps, that is, jump long rather than high. You can place a couple of wider boards side to side on the ground and have your dog jump over them. Another way to change up this training is to send your dog over an obstacle and then call him back to you over the same obstacle.

Training after the Lure

Over

- After your dog responds reliably when lured with a treat, you can stop using the leash and the lure. You use a treat as a reward after your dog performs the trick.

1 Have your dog wait in front of the obstacle while you walk to the side of the obstacle.

2 Say "Over."

3 Move your right hand in the direction you want your dog to jump. This is the hand signal for Over.

- Your dog jumps over the obstacle.

4 When your dog jumps over the obstacle, give your dog a special food treat and praise him.

Note: If your dog does not jump over the obstacle, turn away from your dog for five seconds and then repeat steps 1 to 4. After three unsuccessful attempts, return to training the Over trick with a treat lure.

weave

The Weave trick challenges your dog to walk in between and around your legs, moving from front to back, while you walk forward. Once mastered, this trick is sure to impress just about anyone.

Training the Weave trick requires you and your dog to maintain coordination and balance. For you, the challenge is to manipulate the treat lure behind and around your knees, alternating between right and left, while drawing your dog between your legs toward the treat in your hands. Make sure your dog can see the treat at all times. For your dog, he has to weave between your legs and then around to face you again.

When training the Weave trick, you should work up to taking three steps forward. When your dog knows how to perform the trick, you can take as many steps forward as you wish.

The hand signal for the Weave trick is similar to the path your hands take when luring your dog with a treat. You use your empty hand as a target for your dog to follow and then gradually make the hand signal smaller. With time, your dog will not need to follow your hand to circle in front of you. He will circle back to the front on his own.

Training with a Lure

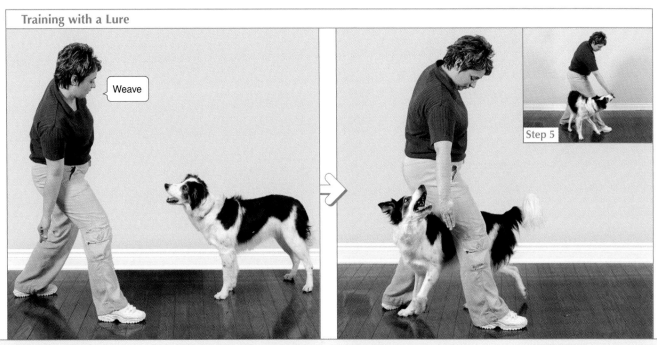

- When you start training your dog to weave, you use a lure to guide your dog. You will most often use a treat as a lure.

1 Start with your dog in the Stand position (page 102) in front of you.

2 With your right foot, take one large step forward.

3 Say the command "Weave."

4 Holding a treat between your fingertips and thumb, position your right hand behind your right knee.

- Your dog walks under your right leg to reach the treat.

5 Slowly move your right hand around your right leg and out in front of you, keeping your hand at knee level.

- Your dog follows the treat and walks out in front of you.

6 Give your dog the treat and praise him.

7 Repeat steps 2 to 6 on your left side.

Tip

What can I try if my dog is hesitant about going under my legs?

If your dog is nervous about going under your legs, try to get him used to the idea of going under your legs before you start training the Weave trick. Simply toss some treats between your legs, making sure that he has no way to get to the treats, which are now behind you, except through your legs.

My dog loves performing the Touch command, so he easily follows my hand. Is this helpful for the Weave trick?

Yes, you can work the Touch command into your training for this trick. With your hand in the same position behind your leg as if you were holding a lure during the Weave training, get your dog to walk under your legs to touch your hand. Instead of luring your dog under your legs with a treat, you reward him with a treat after he has touched your hand. You then continue with the Weave hand signal to complete the trick. For information on the Touch command, see page 123.

Training after the Lure

Weave

- After your dog responds reliably when lured with a treat, use a treat only as a reward after your dog performs the trick.

1 Start with your dog in the Stand position in front of you.

2 With your right foot, take one large step forward.

3 Say the command "Weave."

4 Position your right hand behind your right knee and then move your hand out in front of you. This is the hand signal for Weave.

- Your dog walks under your right leg and then out in front of you.

5 Repeat steps 2 to 4 on your left side.

6 After your dog weaves through both legs, give your dog a special food treat and praise him.

Note: If your dog does not weave, turn away from your dog for five seconds and then repeat steps 1 to 6. After three unsuccessful attempts, return to training the Weave trick with a treat lure.

Chapter 9

As your dog responds more and more reliably to your commands, you can start progressing toward working with your dog off his leash while outdoors. When your dog is able to work with you off his leash, you can confidently take him to an off-leash park to play with other dogs. This chapter also includes information on sports and activities that you can consider participating in with your dog.

Working Off Leash

In this Chapter...

progressing toward off-leash work

Off-leash training, which is conducted outside, teaches your dog to respond to your commands even when he is off his leash and is faced with distractions. Off-leash training helps prepare your dog for playing in off-leash parks and for participating in organized dog sports, such as agility trials. Do not attempt off-leash training until your dog reliably responds to commands indoors and on leash.

When you begin off-leash training, practice in a confined area, such as a fenced yard. You should also keep your dog on a long line that you can step on if he runs off, ignores you or becomes distracted. A long line lets you control your dog, but is not as confining as a leash. When training outside, you must make yourself as exciting as possible to your dog since there are many more distractions outside than there are inside.

When your dog responds at least 80 percent of the time to the Sit, Stand and Down commands and can hold a Stay for up to one minute, you can move off-leash training to a fenced off-leash park. Training in an off-leash park will be challenging for your dog as he will be exposed to even more distractions.

Sit, Stand and Down Commands

1 Attach a long line to your dog's collar and have a helper stand near your dog, loosely holding the long line.

2 Stand at least six feet away from your dog.

3 Say the command "Sit," "Stand" or "Down."

4 When your dog complies, go to your dog and give him a special food treat.

- If your dog does not comply, say the command again with more emphasis. When your dog complies, praise him but do not give him a food treat.

Note: If your dog still does not comply, move closer to your dog and then repeat steps 3 and 4.

5 Repeat steps 2 to 4 four times, changing your location and the command you say each time.

Tip

How do I keep my dog interested in me, even when he is faced with distractions?

One way to make yourself exciting to your dog is to keep him guessing. For example, when working on one of the commands described below, position yourself in different locations and at different distances from your dog. You may want to give a command while sitting at a picnic table or when leaning against a tree. When working on the Stay command, create your own distraction by running in a circle, jumping up and down or playing with a child.

How can I progress when training my dog to hold a Stay off leash?

Before working on the Stay command off leash, your dog should reliably hold a Stay when he is on leash and faced with distractions. When you are training the Stay command off leash, remain close to your dog initially and avoid leaving him in the Stay position for longer than his interest level will allow. When he responds reliably off leash, gradually increase your distance from your dog and reduce how often you step in to give him a food treat while he stays in position.

Stay Command

1 Attach a long line to your dog's collar.

2 Standing in front of your dog, say the command "Sit," "Stand" or "Down" to get your dog into position. Then say the command "Stay."

3 Move six feet away from your dog, with the long line on the ground between you and your dog.

4 While your dog stays, give him a special food treat and then move slightly farther away.

5 Repeat step 4 two more times. After the second time, release your dog instead of giving him a treat.

Note: If your dog moves out of position, move closer to your dog and then repeat steps 2 to 5, standing closer to your dog.

CONTINUED...

progressing toward off-leash work *(continued)*

In addition to participating in organized dog sports or taking your dog to an off-leash park, another reason to practice off-leash training is to keep your dog safe in potentially dangerous situations. If your dog runs away from you, escapes from your yard or pulls the leash out of your hand, you will still have some control over your dog if you have worked on off-leash training.

Two more commands to work on during off-leash training are the Come command and the Heel command. Before training your dog to come or heel when off leash, your dog should reliably come when you call him and not pull on the leash when walking. Also, make sure that your dog is properly socialized so he is not aggressive toward other dogs or people. When training the Heel command off leash, visualize where you want your dog to be when he is heeling. Give him a treat only when he reaches the spot you have visualized.

When your dog is coming to you 80 percent of the time and is heeling well off leash, you can move your training to another safe setting with more distractions.

Come Command

1 Attach a long line to your dog's collar.

2 Stand 10 feet from your dog, with the long line on the ground between you and your dog.

3 Say your dog's name.

4 Say the command "Come."

• When your dog starts to move toward you, praise him.

Note: If your dog does not move toward you, make yourself more interesting to him. For example, turn and run away from him to entice him to chase you.

5 When your dog reaches you, touch his collar, give him a special food treat and praise him enthusiastically.

6 Continue to practice, gradually increasing your distance from your dog, until your dog is coming straight to you eight out of ten times.

Tip

What else can I try if my dog struggles with the Come command off leash?

If you have more than one dog, introduce a bit of envy into your training. Give a treat to the other dog, making sure that the dog you are training notices the treat and attention he is not getting. You can also wait your dog out by stepping on his line until he pays attention to you. After he does so, give him plenty of praise.

How do I avoid becoming frustrated with my dog when he does not come when called?

Responding to the Come command can be difficult because of the many distractions your dog is exposed to outdoors. Remember that coming when called is simply a matter of developing a good habit. When your dog does not come, take it as a sign that more practice is needed. When your dog does come, treat him as if he is the best dog in the world.

Heel

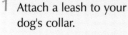

1. Attach a leash to your dog's collar.

2. Standing with the dog on your left side, drape the leash across the front of your body and allow the loop of the leash to hang over your right shoulder.

3. Say the command "Heel" and then walk forward with your dog.

4. When your dog is heeling, use your right hand to give him a treat randomly.

5. Continue to practice until your dog is comfortable heeling with the leash over your shoulder.

- Make sure you vary your direction and speed when your dog is heeling. This ensures your dog is paying attention to you and will stay with you no matter where you go.

Introduction to off-leash parks

When your dog is at least six months old and knows to come when you call him, consider taking him to an off-leash park. Also called dog runs or dog parks, off-leash parks provide controlled open space in which dogs can shed their leash and exercise and socialize with you, other dogs and other dog owners. Check with your local dog-license bureau to find out the locations of off-leash parks or parks with designated off-leash areas.

Daily exercise can improve your dog's behavior at home and regular visits to an off-leash park are a good way to get that exercise. However, you should use caution when visiting an off-leash park. Make sure that the off-leash area is completely fenced in and pay attention to the park's posted rules and warnings. Remember that your dog is just one of many dogs and you probably do not know the other dogs well enough to anticipate their behavior. Observe your dog closely to prevent him from mimicking any poor behavior of other dogs or from getting involved in fighting or other aggressive behavior.

Benefits of Off-Leash Parks

- Off-leash parks allow your dog to exercise safely off his leash.

  Note: You must keep your dog's leash with you at all times in the park, in case you need to get control of your dog.

- Playing in an off-leash park provides mental stimulation for your dog.

- Off-leash parks allow your dog to socialize and play with other dogs.

- Dog owners can meet other people at off-leash parks who share their interest in dogs and dog issues.

- Even while socializing with other dog owners, make sure you watch and control your dog at all times in the park.

Tip

My dog is a little withdrawn around other dogs. Should I avoid off-leash parks?

Some dogs are intimidated or otherwise out of their element in large groups. Look for smaller play groups in which your dog can exercise and socialize.

Should I take my puppy to an off-leash park?

Off-leash parks are not suitable for puppies under six months of age. Look for smaller play groups with puppies around his age. Also, remember that socialization for your dog involves more than just running around with other dogs. See page 72 for more information on socializing your dog.

Should I be concerned about my dog picking up any diseases from other dogs at the off-leash park?

Any time a large group of dogs play together in a relatively confined environment, there are risks that diseases will spread. However, do not let that possibility prohibit you and your dog from visiting an off-leash park. Check with your veterinarian to find out what to be concerned about before you head for the park.

Pitfalls of Off-Leash Parks

- Some dogs do not play nicely with other dogs.

- If your dog is being bothersome to other dogs, you should take your dog home and return at another time.

- All owners must control their dogs to ensure everyone has a pleasant experience at the park. Owners who do not control their dogs may be asked to leave.

- Some dogs may not have experience interacting with children.

- If you must bring children to an off-leash park, keep them close to you at all times.

- Children should never approach a dog without first asking permission from the dog's owner.

tips for visiting off-leash parks

Going to an off-leash park should be an enjoyable experience for you, your dog and other dogs and their owners. There are things you can do before and during your visit to make sure your off-leash park time is successful.

Before you enter the park, your dog should be on leash. Resist the temptation to give him an off-leash head start and run free into the park. Instead, keep him safe from traffic around the park by leading him on leash to the park entrance. When you arrive at the off-leash area, take a moment to have your dog sit

and observe the activity inside so that you and your dog have an idea of how other dogs are playing.

Once inside the park, immediately take off your dog's leash. After sitting outside the park watching other dogs play, your dog is ready to have some fun. If you are nervous about letting your dog off leash, you should not visit an off-leash park. Take him somewhere else to play if you prefer to keep him on leash. Also, if your dog wears a chain collar, head halter or body harness, remove it so he does not get tangled up.

- Keep your dog on his leash until you are inside the off-leash park. Keeping your dog on his leash keeps him safe from cars and keeps him under your control in the parking lot.

- Use the Let's Go command (see page 110) to walk your dog calmly into the park. Do not allow your dog to pull you into the park.

- The first time you and your dog visit an off-leash park, you should try to visit when the park is not too busy.

- Weekday afternoons are usually less-busy times at off-leash parks.

- When you arrive at the park, take a moment to have your dog sit outside the park and watch the other dogs play. Both you and your dog can use this time to evaluate the other dogs inside.

Tip

When can I be sure my dog is ready for an off-leash park?

When your dog reliably comes to you when you call him while he is off leash at home, he is ready to venture into a public off-leash area. Until your dog comes when called at home without hesitation, you should not feel confident that he will do so with the many distractions of an off-leash park. If your dog does not come when called while inside an off-leash park, go and get him yourself. To continue calling without him responding only teaches him not to listen to you.

What should I do when my dog eliminates while inside an off-leash park?

An off-leash park is a play area for other dogs and dog owners. Be considerate of other park visitors and clean up after your dog as soon as possible after he eliminates. You should be watching your dog closely while inside the park, so you will know where and when he eliminates. Plastic grocery bags are good to use for the waste. You are sure to find trash receptacles throughout the park.

- As soon as you get inside the park, say the command "Sit" and then take off your dog's leash as his reward for sitting.

  Note: If you do not remove your dog's leash, he may feel threatened and become aggressive toward other dogs.

- Keep your dog moving while in the park. Your dog cannot get into trouble if he is busy running and playing.

- During your time at the park, call your dog to you regularly and praise him enthusiastically each time he comes.

- When you are ready to leave, go and get your dog instead of calling him to you. You do not want him to feel punished for coming to you.

- Re-attach your dog's leash to his collar before you leave the park.

things to do at off-leash parks

Going to an off-leash park is a time to have fun, play games and be together with your dog. An off-leash park also is a good spot to practice commands with your dog. The park activity presents many distractions that you and your dog can work with.

If you and your dog play games at the park, however, look for an area of the park that has fewer distractions. For example, if you have toys that you bring with you, take your dog to an area where other dogs are less likely to try to join in the fun and take the toys for their own.

Do not forget to reserve some activity time for your dog to enjoy the company of other dogs. Always make sure you know where your dog is and how well he is playing with the other dogs. Be prepared to call your dog away and take him home if he refuses to play nicely with other dogs. If other dogs are not playing nicely with your dog, try another area of the park before you decide to take him home.

- You can work on commands with your dog while you are at the off-leash park. This allows your dog to practice commands in a high-distraction area.

Note: An off-leash park is not a good place to teach new commands to your dog. You should always train new commands in a low-distraction area.

- Play games, such as Hide and Seek (see page 140), with your dog while you are at the off-leash park.

- If you choose to play games that use toys, such as Fetch (see page 142) or Tug (see page 144), be sure you are in an area where other dogs will not be tempted to steal the toy away from your dog.

Tip

My dog seems to enjoy a little rough play with other dogs. Is this okay?

Monitor what kind of rough play your dog is participating in. If your dog, or a dog he is playing with, rises up on his hind legs to another dog, as if in a boxing position, you should deter that behavior. A few innocent jousts may be okay, but constant rough play like this can lead to an injury. If you see your dog repeatedly assuming this position against another dog, move him away and redirect his attention to a new activity. You do not want the boxing or other rough-play behavior to get out of control.

Do off-leash parks have play equipment for dogs on site?

Some off-leash parks have agility obstacles set up so that dogs can work on agility training in a safe setting. You may discover that your dog is quite adept at conquering these obstacles, perhaps enough to consider additional agility training. For more information on agility, see page 195.

- Allow your dog to play with other dogs in the park.
- When your dog plays with another dog, respect the wishes of the other dog's owner. All dogs do not like the same type of playing.

Note: If your dog is too energetic for another dog, move with your dog to another area of the park.

- Make sure you monitor your dog's play with other dogs.
- When dogs play, they alternate roles. Sometimes one dog chases while the other is chased and then they switch.

- If your dog is always the dog being chased, there is a good chance your dog is not playing but is being bullied by the other dog.
- If you feel your dog is being bullied, move with your dog to another area of the park.

sports and activities for your dog

There are a wide variety of dog sports and organized activities that you can participate in with your dog once your dog has learned the basic training commands. Activities and events are often sponsored by kennel clubs or other organizations, with the rules for each event depending on the sponsor. When choosing activities you want to participate in with your dog, you should consider your dog's skills and current ability level.

Obedience and Conformation

Competitive Obedience

Competitive obedience events involve you and your dog completing a series of exercises, while being judged on the precision of the performance. There are various levels of competition, with awards at each level. At lower levels, basic obedience skills are performed on a leash. At higher levels of competition, more advanced obedience skills are judged, such as jumping over hurdles and off-leash precision heeling.

Dogs of all ages and types can participate in competitive obedience events, though only purebreds are eligible for American Kennel Club events.

Rally Obedience

Rally obedience, also known as Rally-O, is a relaxed form of obedience competition that emphasizes teamwork between the dog and his owner. Rally obedience is a fun way to introduce your dog to competitive events. In a Rally-O competition, you and your dog move through stations that contain a series of obedience activities. Rally-O competitions are designed to be inclusive, so that dogs and owners of all abilities can participate in a fun relationship building activity.

Conformation

In conformation events, dogs are judged based on how well they meet their breed standard. A breed standard is a written description of the ideal dog in each breed, including qualities such as body length, coat color, eye color, head shape and temperament.

To compete in a conformation event your dog must be a registered purebred and must be an excellent example of his breed.

Organized Sports

Agility Trials

Agility trials are timed events in which you take your dog through an obstacle course. The obstacle course includes activities such as jumping over hurdles, running through tunnels and weaving through poles. Your dog is judged based on his speed and how well he keeps on the course.

Dogs of all types can participate in agility trials. In order to compete, your dog should enjoy physical activity and be well trained in obedience, since he will not be on a leash during the competition.

Musical Freestyle

If you are a creative dog owner who wants to demonstrate your dog's skills in an expressive format, you can compete in a musical freestyle competition. In musical freestyle, you and your dog perform a choreographed routine that highlights your dog's obedience skills and abilities. The routine is set to music and performed in costume. Musical freestyle competitions can be compared to dance competitions or pairs figure skating events, with you and your dog judged on creativity and skill.

Flying Disc

In flying disc competitions, you throw Frisbees® for your dog to catch. Flying disc competitions can consist of catch and retrieve events and freestyle events.

In a catch and retrieve event, you and your dog try to throw and catch as many Frisbees® as possible within a time limit. The team that completes the most catches wins the event.

In freestyle events, dogs and owners perform choreographed routines that consist of tricks displaying a variety of throws and catches with a Frisbee®. The routines are usually set to music and are popular competitions that are fun to watch.

Flyball

Flyball competitions are relay races in which teams consisting of four dogs compete against each other. In a flyball competition, each dog races over a set of hurdles and then steps on a board to launch a ball into the air. The dog catches the ball and races back over the hurdles to return to the start so the next dog on the team can complete the same course. The first team to have each of its four dogs complete the course wins the competition.

CONTINUED...

sports and activities
for your dog
(continued)

Breed Specific Competitions

Earthdog Trials

Earthdog trials are designed for dogs such as small terriers and Dachshunds that were originally bred to hunt animals like badgers and rats hiding in tunnels or dens. Quarry, which may be a live caged rat or an artificial animal, is placed in a tunnel or den. The dogs are judged on their ability to track the quarry and get at the quarry by barking, digging and scratching.

Field Trials

Field trials allow hunting dogs to demonstrate their skills of tracking and retrieving birds. Also showcased is the dog's ability to flush, which refers to "flushing" birds out of their hiding spots, and pointing, which refers to the dog pointing their nose toward the direction of the bird's hiding spot.

Tracking Trials

If your dog is skilled at following scents, you can train him to participate in a tracking trial. Tracking trials are challenging outdoor competitions in which dogs compete to see who is the best tracker. Dogs of all types who enjoy following scent can participate in most tracking events.

Herding Trials

Herding dogs, such as Australian Shepherds, Collies, Border Collies and Sheepdogs can participate in herding trials to demonstrate their ability to herd livestock such as cattle, ducks, goats or sheep. In a herding trial, dogs must usually move livestock through a series of gates and into a confinement area.

Lure Coursing

Sight hounds, such as Greyhounds, Whippets, Deerhounds and Afghan Hounds can compete in lure coursing competitions. In these competitions, dogs chase a lure around an outdoor course while being judged on their enthusiasm, speed and endurance.

Sled Dog Racing

In sled dog racing, a team of dogs pulls a sled and driver, who is also known as a musher. Sled dog races can vary from one mile to over 1000 miles long, and are open to all types of dogs.

Breed Specific Competitions (continued)

Schutzhund Trials

Schutzhund is a German word that translates to "protection dog." A schutzhund trial is a specialized competition for dog breeds often used in police work, such as German Shepherds, Dobermans and Boxers. In schutzhund trials, dogs compete in tracking, obedience and protection activities. A dog must have an extremely stable temperament and be taught by a qualified individual to participate in schutzhund trials.

Drafting

In drafting competitions, dogs pull an item, such as a cart, wagon, sled or log through a course. Working dogs such as Newfoundlands, Bernese Mountain Dogs, Great Pyrenees and Greater Swiss Mountain Dogs commonly compete in drafting competitions, although smaller breeds can also participate. During a drafting competition, dogs must cooperate while being hitched up to equipment and be able to back up and change speeds while pulling the equipment.

Public Service Activities

Therapy Dogs

Therapy dogs, also called visiting dogs, bring comfort and companionship to people who are confined to hospitals or nursing homes. By improving the emotional well-being of patients, therapy dogs can help to promote healing.

To become a therapy dog, your dog must have an extremely stable temperament and be thoroughly trained.

Search and Rescue

Search and rescue is challenging work that requires dogs to enter into dangerous areas with their owners in order to save people who are injured or lost. For example, search and rescue dogs are used to find people who have been buried in avalanches.

To become a search and rescue dog, training begins when the dog is a puppy.

Chapter 10

This chapter addresses some of the most common problem behaviors that dogs exhibit, such as begging, jumping up on people or furniture, destructive chewing or digging, chasing cars and much more. You will find helpful hints and information to help you deal with many problem behaviors. This chapter also includes information on some of the special needs of aging dogs.

Working With Problem Behaviors

In this Chapter...

begging

Begging is an unwanted behavior that you should try to discourage in your dog. This behavior may include actions such as staring, pawing at you or others, whining, drooling or any other attempt to solicit food.

Begging becomes a problem when you give in to your dog's demands, which reinforces his begging behavior. It can also be troublesome when you do not stop your dog from begging. For example, a dog that paws at you to get to your toast can very easily knock over the cup of coffee beside your breakfast.

The best response to a begging dog is to never give in to his demands. For example, if your dog is begging for your food, you can ignore his begging or use the Settle command to get him to lie quietly. Giving your dog a stuffed Kong™ to chew on while you eat will also keep your dog from begging for your food. You should never give your dog table scraps from your plate as this will reinforce his begging.

- Dogs beg to try to obtain the food you are eating.

- Begging is a demanding behavior you should try to discourage in your dog.

- You should not feed your dog from the table. Feeding your dog from the table, even occasionally, will reinforce begging.

- Until you have trained your dog not to beg, put him in his crate before you start eating.

- Keeping your dog in his crate removes the dog from the situation and prevents him from having the opportunity to beg.

- You can give your dog a stuffed Kong™ to chew while he is in the crate.

Tip

Is begging always for food?

Your dog may also beg for a pet, a scratch, a car ride or a walk. For example, if your dog is pacing around and looking at you expectantly, he may be begging for a walk. If you immediately take him for a walk, you are giving in to a demanding dog. Instead, make him earn his walk by obeying a few commands first, such as the Sit, Down and Come commands.

Can I feed my dog human food?

Yes, but you should not do so from the table, which encourages and rewards begging. Instead, include human food as part of his daily ration in his food bowl or his Kong™. Remember that foods that are bad for you, such as fried foods or sweets, are also bad for your dog. Examples of good human food to give him are cottage cheese, peanut butter, pieces of vegetables such as carrots and green beans, pieces of fruit such as apples or grapes and cuts of lean meat.

Training by Ignoring the Dog

1 If your dog begs by staring or drooling, you should ignore him.

- Ignoring your dog teaches him that begging will not result in food or attention.

2 When your dog is not begging, praise him.

Training by Using the Settle and Stay Commands

1 If your dog begs by whining, barking or pawing at you or the table, use the Settle command (page 106) followed by the Stay command (page 108) before you begin eating to have your dog lie down quietly while you eat.

2 When your dog is quiet, give him a stuffed Kong™ to chew.

3 When you finish eating, release your dog from the Settle and Stay position.

jumping up on people

When a dog jumps up on someone, he considers this to be a friendly gesture. However, most people view a dog jumping up on them as annoying, especially when entering the house carrying groceries or when wearing nice clothes. A dog jumping up on people can also be dangerous. The dog could knock a person over and cause injury, especially children and the elderly.

To correct this behavior, you can use the Sit command. A dog cannot sit and jump up on people at the same time. When your dog learns that his sit will be rewarded and his jumping up will be ignored, over time he will choose to sit rather than jump up.

In order for your training to be effective, your entire family and all visitors must be consistent in ignoring your dog when he jumps up. If visitors say that they do not mind when your dog jumps up, try saying "Can you help me train my dog by not allowing him to jump up on you?" Visitors will then feel like they are helping you out.

You should try to practice this exercise five times per training session.

Jumping Up on the Owner

1 Open your front door and enter your house.

2 When your dog jumps up, quickly turn away from him and walk away.

- Do not greet or pet your dog.

3 Return to your dog.

4 Say the command "Sit." For more information on the Sit command, see page 100.

5 When your dog is sitting, give him a treat and praise him.

- If your dog does not sit, repeat steps 2 to 5.

Tip

How can I prevent my puppy from jumping up on people?

First, you should never encourage your puppy to jump up to receive attention. You should always have your puppy sit before you give him attention. Also, do not be overly excited when you greet your puppy as this will encourage him to jump up on you.

How can I manage my dog's jumping up on people when we are not training?

You can attach a long line, such as a piece of rope, to your dog's collar. The line should be approximately eight to ten feet long. When someone comes to the door, you can step on the line to prevent your dog from jumping up on the visitor. Once your dog is sitting calmly, you should praise him.

You should only use a long line when you are supervising your dog. Using a long line is especially useful when you are expecting many visitors to arrive in short period of time, such as when you are having a party.

Jumping Up on a Visitor

1 Before the visitor enters your house, attach a leash to your dog's collar.

2 Say the command "Sit."

3 When your dog is sitting, ask the visitor to enter the house.

4 Ask the visitor to approach you and your dog.

5 While your dog is sitting, ask the visitor to give your dog a treat.

• If your dog jumps up, instruct the visitor to turn away from your dog and go back to the entrance. Then repeat steps 4 and 5.

6 While your dog is sitting, you can also give him a treat and praise him.

jumping up on furniture

Allowing your dog to jump up on your furniture is a decision you should make when you first bring him home. To allow him on furniture when you first bring him home and then to take that privilege away later on is confusing and unfair. If you decide to allow your dog on your furniture, it should be by your invitation only. You do not want your dog to have automatic furniture privileges. Rather, invite him for occasional access and he must get off when you tell him "Off." If you decide that you do not want your dog on your furniture, do not invite him up—ever.

To correct your dog when jumping up on furniture, you train him using a long line, stepping on it to prevent him from reaching your furniture and using the Off command. You can also make your furniture unappealing to your dog by placing tinfoil on top of it. Dogs generally do not like to lie on tinfoil. You can also provide him with a comfortable dog bed to lie on in the family area as an alternative to your furniture.

- Dogs jump up on furniture because the furniture is comfortable for them to sit and lie on.

- You should decide when you get your dog whether or not he will be allowed on the furniture.

- If you do not want to allow your dog on the furniture, do not invite him onto the furniture, even when he is a puppy.

- When you are not at home or are unable to supervise your dog, you can make the furniture less appealing to your dog. For example, you can turn up the cushions on the couch or put tinfoil on the furniture. Most dogs do not like to lie on tinfoil.

- You can also make another location more appealing than the furniture, such as providing a comfortable dog bed for your dog to sit and lie on.

Tip

What should I do if my dog will not get off the furniture when I ask him to?

Start by saying the Off command. If your dog does not respond, attach his leash to his collar and guide him off the furniture. Remember to give him verbal praise when he is off the furniture, whether after responding to the Off command or after being guided off. If your dog growls at you when you try to attach his leash or when you try to maneuver him off the furniture, he may have a more serious problem called resource guarding. You must deal with this type of behavior. For information on resource guarding, see page 226.

What else can I do?

Until you have trained your dog to not jump up on furniture uninvited, you can place him in a confinement area where there is no furniture, such as a laundry room. You can also gate off rooms or simply close the doors to rooms that you do not want your dog to have access to until he is trained not to jump up on the furniture.

Training Using the Off Command

Off

Training Using a Long Line

1 When you are at home, you can supervise your dog to ensure he is not jumping up on the furniture uninvited.

2 If your dog jumps up on the furniture uninvited, say the command "Off" and point to the floor.

3 When your dog gets down off the furniture, praise him.

1 When you are able to closely supervise your dog, attach a long line to your dog's collar.

2 If your dog attempts to jump up on the furniture uninvited, step on the long line to prevent him from jumping up on the furniture.

3 When your dog backs away from the furniture, praise him and give him a treat.

destructive chewing

Chewing is a normal dog behavior. However, destructive chewing is an unwanted dog behavior, which occurs when dogs chew shoes, furniture, baseboards and other inappropriate items. Dogs chew to relieve boredom and stress, and to discover more about their surroundings. In particular, young dogs have a compelling need to chew, both for entertainment and to use their new teeth.

To help prevent destructive chewing, make sure your dog has opportunities to chew appropriate things, such as a stuffed Kong™ or other quality chew toy. Also, make sure there are not any items available to

chew that you do not want him to chew, even items you no longer use. For example, if you allow your dog to chew an old pair of shoes, he will likely chew a new pair of shoes, as he cannot differentiate between the two. Exercising your dog, which mentally stimulates him and limits boredom, will also help prevent destructive chewing.

Manage your dog's chewing behavior early on. If you can prevent him from chewing a shoe while he is young, he will be much less likely to chew a shoe when he matures.

- Chewing is a natural, normal dog behavior. Dogs chew for many reasons—to relieve the discomfort of teething, to learn about their surroundings and for fun.

- Chewing becomes a problem when your dog chews inappropriate items such as shoes, clothing, furniture, walls and baseboards.

- To prevent your dog from chewing inappropriate items, such as shoes, socks and pantyhose, make sure the items are put away so he cannot access them.

- Dogs have a natural need to chew. You can provide appropriate items for your dog to chew. For example, provide good quality chew toys such as sterilized bones or Kongs™ stuffed with treats.

Note: To stuff a Kong™, see page 234.

- You should consult your veterinarian before giving your dog completely consumable items, such as pig's ears, cow hooves or rawhide.

Tip

Should I punish my dog when he chews something valuable?

No. Your dog will associate the punishment with you, not with the act of chewing. He will also learn to chew on inappropriate items when you are not around to punish him. Instead, proactively manage your dog's environment and lifestyle so he has only good chewing opportunities. When he chews something inappropriate, clean up the mess and resolve to manage things better next time.

Why has my dog started chewing after becoming housetrained?

Inappropriate chewing often follows housetraining because you supervise your dog less and he has more freedom to move around the house. Confinement, supervision and management should be part of your dog's life for about one year.

- Boredom is a major reason for destructive chewing.

- To prevent boredom, you can provide your dog with opportunities for exercise. This will help ensure your dog gets the physical and mental stimulation he needs.

- A dog that exercises regularly will have less energy for destructive chewing.

- Until you have trained your dog to chew only appropriate items, you can keep him in a secure environment, such as his crate, when you are not home or are unable to supervise him.

- Training your dog to stay in his crate prevents him from accessing and chewing inappropriate items.

- Make sure you provide your dog with appropriate items to chew while he is in the crate.

destructive digging

Digging is a natural, normal behavior for dogs. However, digging becomes destructive when your dog digs holes in inappropriate areas of the yard, such as in the garden or middle of the lawn.

A lack of supervision is one of the most common causes of destructive digging. When you supervise your dog, you can stop the digging behavior so your dog does not have the opportunity to be destructive. If you practice close supervision when your dog is young, it is unlikely that he will pick up the hobby of digging when he is a mature dog.

If your dog is bored, he may dig as a means of stimulation. To prevent boredom, you can provide your dog with opportunities for exercise. Allowing your dog to burn off energy in other ways will help ensure he gets the physical and mental stimulation he needs.

You can also prevent destructive digging by providing your dog with an alternative digging site, such as a designated digging pit where your dog is allowed to dig. You should encourage your dog to dig in the digging pit.

- Digging is a natural, normal dog behavior. Dogs dig for many reasons—to bury items they want to hide, to find a cool place to lie when it is hot outside and for fun.

- Digging becomes destructive when your dog digs in inappropriate areas of the yard, such as in the garden or middle of the lawn.

- Lack of supervision is one of the most common causes of destructive digging.

- When you allow your dog access to the yard, you are giving him the opportunity to dig. You must be there to ensure he does not engage in destructive digging.

- When you go into the house, you should bring your dog into the house as well.

- You should avoid leaving your dog alone outside for extended periods of time.

Tip

How can I encourage my dog to dig in the digging pit?

When your dog is not looking, you can place food treats, toys or bones just under the surface of the soil in the digging pit to encourage your dog to dig in the pit. Tell your dog to "Go to your pit" and walk him to the digging pit. You may need to help him find the items at first. Soon your dog will automatically go to the pit when he wants to dig. Being able to dig is its own reward—the extra items just reinforce that this is a good place to dig.

How can I keep my dog away from forbidden areas?

You can place a visible barrier, such as a fence, chicken wire or boat rope, around a forbidden area. With your dog on a leash, approach the forbidden area. If your dog touches the barrier say "Off" and back away. Repeat this process for a couple of days until you can approach the forbidden area and your dog does not touch the barrier. When he does not touch the barrier, give him a treat and praise him enthusiastically.

- Boredom is another cause of destructive digging.

- To prevent boredom, you can provide your dog with opportunities for exercise. This will ensure your dog gets the physical and mental stimulation he needs.

- A dog that exercises regularly will have less energy for destructive digging.

- Dogs have a natural need to dig. You can provide an appropriate area for your dog to dig, such as a digging pit.

- A digging pit is a designated area in the yard where your dog is allowed to dig. A digging pit can be a pile of sand or soft soil.

- When your dog starts to dig in an inappropriate area of the yard say "Off. Go to your pit." Then walk him over to the pit and encourage him to dig in the pit.

chasing cars or people

Dogs instinctively want to chase moving objects. This behavior can become dangerous if your dog starts to chase after people or moving cars. Until your dog's chasing is under control, you should manage this behavior by always keeping him on a leash.

Training your dog to control his chase instinct requires a great deal of focused observation on your part. You will need to be able to tell just by looking at your dog when he is about to give chase. Once you recognize the telltale signs that your dog is ready to chase, you start the training routine that catches him just before he takes off.

Your goal is to interrupt his chasing behavior and to refocus his attention on you, even if it is just for a fraction of a second at the beginning of training. Be patient. Your dog may not look at you for some time when you begin training. You should continue to train using the steps below until your dog automatically looks at you when he wants to chase an inappropriate object or person.

- Chasing is a natural, normal dog behavior. Dogs instinctively want to chase moving objects.

- Chasing becomes a problem when your dog chases inappropriate objects or people, such as cars or joggers.

- Do not allow your dog to chase inappropriate objects or people. Allowing your dog to chase objects or people could result in serious injury for your dog and the person he is chasing.

- Training your dog using these steps teaches your dog to look at you whenever he wants to chase an inappropriate object or person. Having your dog look at you interrupts the chasing behavior and focuses your dog's attention on you.

- When training your dog not to chase, make sure you work in a safe environment, such as a fenced yard.

- You will need the help of another person to train your dog not to chase.

Tip

My dog is not motivated by food to stop chasing. What else can I do to motivate him?

For some dogs, food may not be as rewarding as the potential for a good chase. Try adding Fetch to the steps below. In step 3, say your dog's name as you bounce a ball to get his attention. In step 4, when your dog looks at you, throw the ball a short distance for him to chase and fetch. Make sure you follow him and hold securely to his leash. When he looks at you instead of chasing, you can reward him with a quick game of Fetch. See page 142 for more information on Fetch.

Are there resources I can use to manage my dog's chasing when we are not training?

Try walking your dog using a head halter. If you see that he is ready to chase an object or person, use the head halter to redirect his head toward you and praise him. Give your dog a treat if he chooses to look at you on his own when an object or person to chase is present.

Willy

1 Attach the leash to your dog's collar.

2 Ask the other person to jog past you and your dog.

Note: The other person should jog outside the range of your dog's leash.

3 Before your dog attempts to chase the other person, say your dog's name once.

4 When your dog looks at you, give him a treat and praise him.

- If your dog does not look at you, run in the opposite direction from the other person. When your dog follows, stop running and repeat steps 3 and 4.

- If your dog starts to chase the other person, ask the person to stop moving. Then repeat steps 3 and 4.

5 Repeat steps 2 to 4 ten times in fifteen minutes.

excessive barking

Barking is an acceptable behavior for your dog under controlled conditions. You want your dog to bark when danger is imminent, but the way you respond to other types of barking will go a long way toward preventing or encouraging excessive barking.

Excessive barking is barking for inappropriate reasons or for an extended period of time. Ironically, your attempts to stop this unwanted behavior may inadvertently reward your dog. If you comfort him, you reinforce his barking and any behavior that is reinforced will increase. If you yell at him, he may interpret that as, "We are barking together!"

This attention is also reinforcing to your dog. Even though you are angry, he appreciates angry attention over no attention at all.

You can control your dog's excessive barking by training the Shush command, which he will associate with being quiet. With this command, you can prevent your dog from barking at every movement outside your home, leaving him the opportunity to bark in those situations where you want him to bark. Most importantly, teach your dog consistently that you never want him to bark excessively.

- Barking is a natural, normal dog behavior. Barking is one of the ways that dogs communicate. Your dog may bark to alert you to a situation, show excitement, make a request or let you know that he is bored.

- Barking becomes a problem when your dog barks for inappropriate reasons or for extended periods of time.

- If your dog barks excessively, do not comfort him. Comforting your dog gives him extra attention for barking.

- If your dog barks excessively, do not shout at him. Your dog may think you are barking along with him.

Tip

Are certain breeds of dogs more prone to barking than other breeds?

Some breeds bark more than other breeds. If barking really bothers you, you should investigate whether the breed you are going to choose to bring into your home has been bred for barking. If you select a dog from one of these breeds, practicing the Shush command will teach him to respond to that command by being quiet. Even with breeds that are more prone to barking, you can still work with your dog to make sure his barking does not get out of control.

Is there another way for me to control my dog's excessive barking without me being around to give the Shush command?

Yes, you can train your dog to bark on command. Then, if you rarely use that command, you will limit his problem barking. You can use the Speak command to train your dog to bark when you ask him to. Using the Speak command with dogs that exhibit excessive barking behavior may give you some control over that behavior. For more information about the Speak command, see page 158.

The Shush Command

Shush

- You can use the Shush command to train your dog to stop barking on command.

1 Place a treat in your right hand and close your hand into a fist.

2 Stand in front of your dog.

3 Say the command "Shush."

4 With your fingers facing forward, place your right hand close to your dog's nose and allow him to sniff your hand.

- Since your dog cannot sniff and bark at the same time, your dog is quiet.

5 After your dog has been quiet for approximately five seconds, give your dog the treat and praise him.

- Once your dog associates the command "Shush" with being quiet, you can use the command to control the different types of excessive barking (pages 214 to 215).

CONTINUED...

excessive
barking *(continued)*

Of the four most common types of barking, alarm barking and excitement barking are generally acceptable as long as they do not become excessive. The other two types of barking, request barking and boredom barking, are not acceptable and should be discouraged at all times.

For any type of excessive barking, remember that your dog is more likely to bark in his own environment, such as when he hears or sees something unfamiliar. By exercising him and getting him out of his environment, he will be more likely to rest when he is at home.

Request barking occurs when your dog barks to obtain an item or attention, such as food, a walk or a toy. Fulfilling his request then rewards his barking. When your dog barks at you for something, ignore him until he stops. When he stops barking and finds something else to do, then give him your attention.

Boredom barking occurs when your dog is bored, lonely or isolated, often when he is left alone outside for extended periods of time. One way to control boredom barking is exercise. A tired dog is a happy dog.

Alarm Barking

Excitement Barking

- Alarm barking occurs when your dog wants to alert you to a situation, such as a stranger approaching your house.
- Most people find alarm barking acceptable as long as the barking does not become excessive.

- If alarm barking becomes excessive, allow your dog to bark a few times to alert you. Then use the Come command (page 116) to call him to you, followed by the Shush command (page 213) to tell your dog to stop barking.

- Excitement barking occurs when your dog is excited by a situation, such as when you return home from work or when he is playing with another dog.
- Most people find excitement barking acceptable as long as it does not become excessive.

- If excitement barking becomes excessive, you can use the Settle command (page 106) to have your dog settle down for 30 seconds. Using the Settle command interrupts your dog's barking and helps reduce his excitement level.

Tip

My dog still request barks at me. What else can I do?

When your dog barks at you for an item or attention, you can make him perform some commands. Performing a command disrupts the barking and gets his attention on something else. For example, you can ask him to perform the Come command, followed by the Sit command and then the Down command. When he does, he will have earned the item or attention that he wants.

I keep my dog indoors while I am at work but my neighbors have told me he barks a lot during the day. What can I do?

Excessive barking can be a real concern if you have close neighbors, for example if you live in an apartment building. In these close quarters, your dog is likely to bark at some nearby sound or activity. Creating some background noise, such as from a radio, or blocking access to a window may prevent him from hearing or seeing most distractions. To prevent boredom barking while alone during the day, make sure he has a stuffed Kong™ or other appropriate toy to chew on.

Request Barking

Boredom Barking

- Request barking occurs when your dog barks to obtain an item or attention. For example, your dog may bark when he wants food or a toy.

- You should not reward your dog for request barking by giving him what he wants. This will only reinforce his request barking.

- When your dog request barks, ignore him. When he stops barking, give him your attention again.

- You can also use the Shush command to tell your dog to stop barking.

- Boredom barking occurs when your dog is bored, lonely or isolated. Boredom barking often occurs when your dog is left alone outside for extended periods of time.

- To prevent boredom, you should provide your dog with opportunities for exercise. This will help ensure that your dog gets the physical and mental stimulation he needs.

- To prevent loneliness and isolation, you should not leave your dog alone outside for extended periods of time.

separation anxiety

Like humans, dogs are social creatures that like companionship. When some dogs are left alone, they can experience separation anxiety. Separation anxiety can cause various levels of stressful and panicky behavior by your dog, such as barking, panting, pacing and clawing or other destructive acts.

Dogs can exhibit behavior that is representative of separation anxiety when the owner is at home. For example, if the dog starts to pant and pace when their owner puts on their coat and picks up their car keys, he is showing signs of separation anxiety.

Behavior that indicates separation anxiety can also occur when the owner is away from home. For example, the owner comes home to discover the trim around the back door clawed to pieces.

Every dog has a level of stress that they are able to handle. A dog's ability to handle stress is determined by both his genetics and past experience. While any dog can experience separation anxiety, a dog that came from an animal shelter or was previously abandoned may be more susceptible to having negative associations with being left alone, which may lead to separation anxiety.

What is Separation Anxiety?

- Separation anxiety refers to feelings of stress and panic your dog experiences when left alone.

- If your dog pants, paces, barks excessively or becomes destructive when left alone, he may be experiencing separation anxiety.

- If you think your dog is experiencing separation anxiety, there are several ways you can manage his behavior.

Managing Separation Anxiety

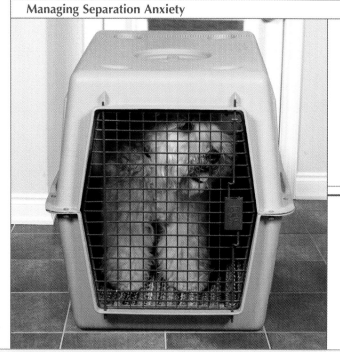

- Keep your dog in a secure environment, such as his crate, when you are not home.

- Keeping your dog in his crate prevents him from hurting himself or damaging your home.

- Most dogs are less anxious in their crate because the crate is a small, familiar environment. If your dog paces when he is anxious, crating him will limit his pacing and prevent his anxiety from escalating.

Tip

Are there resources I can use to manage my dog's separation anxiety?

If you leave your dog alone for regular extended periods of time, such as when going to work, you can enroll him in a dog day care. Before dropping off your dog at one of these facilities, check it out carefully and let the operators know of your dog's separation anxiety. You can also hire a dog walker to pick up your dog from your home and exercise him while you are at work. Again, remember to let the dog walker know of your dog's separation anxiety.

My dog did serious damage to my home while I was out. What should I do?

Repair or clean up the damage. You should never punish your dog when he makes a mess while you are out. He will associate the correction with you coming home, not with the damage he has done, potentially increasing his separation anxiety. Instead, manage how you set up your dog's environment more carefully while you are out, such as by crating your dog.

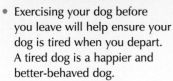

- Exercising your dog before you leave will help ensure your dog is tired when you depart. A tired dog is a happier and better-behaved dog.

- Exercising your dog throughout the day will help ensure he does not have an excess amount of energy stored up, which could increase his feelings of anxiety.

- You should make your departures from home and arrivals at home as uneventful as possible.

- Behave in a calm and relaxed manner when you leave your home and when you return.

- Acting concerned when you leave or overly excited when you return will only increase your dog's feelings of anxiety.

CONTINUED...

separation anxiety (continued)

Few dogs enjoy being left alone, but you can train your dog to accept being on his own and overcome separation anxiety as much as possible.

Training your dog to overcome his separation anxiety requires a predictable departure routine, leaving him alone for only as long as his anxiety threshold will allow. With a predictable routine, your dog will be less anxious because he knows what to expect when you leave.

The training session involves brief departures and quick returns. Upon your return, ignore panicky behavior and only reward calm behavior. You can extend the length of the time you are away as your dog grows more comfortable with your departures. Eventually, add a stuffed Kong™ to the routine. By giving your dog a stuffed Kong™, he learns to associate being alone with enjoying a special, tasty treat. For information on how to stuff a Kong™, see page 234.

When you must leave your dog for long periods, you should manage your dog's separation anxiety. Managing your dog's separation anxiety is completely separate from training him to tolerate being alone. For more information about managing separation anxiety, see page 216.

Training to Overcome Separation Anxiety - Part 1

- You should establish a departure routine for your training sessions. For example, your routine can include putting on your coat and then picking up your car keys before you leave.

- When training to overcome separation anxiety, do not put your dog in his crate.

1 Tell your dog in a calm voice that you are leaving.

2 Perform your departure routine and then leave the house.

3 Wait five seconds and then re-enter the house.

4 If your dog is calm, quietly praise him.

- If your dog is anxious, ignore him until he calms down.

5 Repeat steps 1 to 4 for five minutes.

6 Repeat steps 1 to 5 three times per day.

- Once your dog is comfortable with brief absences, you can gradually increase the time you are away until you can leave the house for five minutes.

Tip

What should I do when my dog shows signs of anxiety during training in Part 1?

If your dog is anxious when you return as part of the training routine, ignore him until he calms down. Then give him your attention by practicing commands and rewarding him with food for positive behavior.

Training my dog to overcome his separation anxiety is not working. What should I do?

When your dog's separation anxiety is serious, you may want to seek help from a trained professional, such as a certified animal behaviorist, qualified dog trainer or veterinarian. A professional can help you work with your dog's behavior, possibly introducing medication to the separation anxiety treatment plan.

Can I leave a stuffed Kong™ with my dog when I go to work?

You want to pair your departure with good things such as a Kong™, but only as part of the training and not as a management strategy for leaving your dog for long periods of time. In training, treats increase your dog's ability to be alone. If you give your dog treats while you are away and he panics, he associates the treat with his feelings of panic.

Training to Overcome Separation Anxiety - Part 2

- When your dog is comfortable being alone for five minutes, you can use food to help train him to be alone for longer periods.

1 Ten minutes before you leave, stuff a Kong™ with treats and place it where your dog cannot reach it.

Note: Preparing the Kong™ 10 minutes before you leave builds up your dog's anticipation for the Kong™.

2 Perform your departure routine.

3 Give your dog the Kong™ and then leave the house.

4 Wait six minutes and then re-enter the house.

5 Ignore your dog for five minutes.

6 After five minutes, greet your dog in a calm manner.

- If your dog is anxious, return to training Part 1.

7 Pick up the Kong™ and put it away.

- You can gradually increase the time you are away until you can leave the house for 30 minutes. Most separation anxiety problems occur within 20 minutes after you leave.

aggression toward people

When a dog shows aggression toward people, this aggression usually takes the form of biting, but may be preceded by warning signs such as hard stares and growling. A dog bite is often the result of a number of stress factors in a particular situation. Stress factors are different for every dog. Knowing your dog's stress factors and helping him to deal with his stress factors in a positive way can help prevent your dog from biting.

Bite Threshold

Every dog has a bite threshold, which refers to the level of stress a dog can handle before the dog bites. When stress factors build up and push the dog over his bite threshold, a bite may occur. When a bite occurs, the owner is often shocked because he never noticed the dog displaying signs of aggression before, but even the most loving and gentle dog may bite in certain situations.

Some dogs have a higher bite threshold than others. Dogs with a higher bite threshold can tolerate much of what life throws their way. Dogs with a lower bite threshold have more difficulty coping with unexpected circumstances and may respond to a stressful situation by biting.

Stress Factors

You should observe your dog to determine what his stress factors are. You can then watch for and reduce these stress factors to decrease the chances of a bite occurring. Stress factors are different for every dog and can include going to new places and meeting new people or certain types of people, such as children or men with facial hair. Other stress factors could include sudden movements, loud noises, health problems, pain or social problems such as resource guarding. For information on resource guarding, see page 226.

Managing Your Dog's Stress

If your dog becomes stressed, you can utilize your dog's basic obedience training to help manage his stress. If your dog is responding to a stressful situation with unwanted behavior, use a command such as Down (page 104) or Settle (page 106) to get him to relax. By performing the command, your dog focuses on the command instead of on what is stressing him. If your dog continues to seem overwhelmed when in stressful situations, consider hiring an animal behaviorist who can help you find out what stresses your dog and will work with you to help your dog overcome that stress.

Preventing Aggression with Socialization

Early and ongoing socialization is the best way to prevent aggression toward people. For information on socialization, see pages 72 to 77. A puppy who has had positive experiences when visiting new places and being handled by different people is more likely to mature into a well-adjusted, confident dog who has a higher bite threshold and can tolerate unfamiliar situations and people without resorting to using his teeth.

When socializing your dog, expose him to different environments, maintaining control of him when he is first introduced to unfamiliar settings. Allow him to meet many types of people, especially children and others who look different than you. Your goal is to have your dog experience all sorts of new things and people in a positive manner.

When a Bite Occurs

If your dog does bite, you should consult a certified animal behaviorist or qualified dog trainer to help you work with your dog to prevent future aggression. You should also take your dog to a veterinarian to determine if your dog has any health problems, since illness and pain can be stress factors. The veterinarian may prescribe medications to control your dog's stress as part of a behavioral treatment plan.

You should take any act of aggressive behavior by your dog seriously. Do not fall into the common trap of making excuses for your dog. Instead, seek out the advice of your veterinarian, an animal behaviorist or a qualified dog trainer. If you ignore the first act of aggression, it may not be the last.

aggression toward other dogs

When a dog shows aggression toward another dog, this aggression usually takes the form of fighting, but may be preceded by warning signs such as hard stares and growling. A number of factors play a role in determining whether a dog will act aggressively toward another dog. These factors include the dog's age, gender and level of socialization.

Social Rank and Aggression

When two dogs meet, the dogs may try to determine their social rank. When one dog assumes a higher status and the other dog accepts this, the rank of the dogs is determined for that particular place and time. When both dogs want to assume the same status, however, aggression may occur. Dogs that are the same sex, size and age are more likely to see each other as rivals and show signs of aggression.

Dogs ranging in age from six months to two years old are more likely to engage in fighting and other aggressive behavior because they are still young. The young dog's immaturity may lead to misunderstandings with other dogs.

Preventing Aggression with Socialization

Early and ongoing socialization is the best defense against aggression toward other dogs. For information on socialization, see pages 72 to 77. Start as soon as possible to get your dog accustomed to seeing other dogs in a variety of venues at different times. If you shelter your dog from other dogs while he is a puppy, he will be more likely to act aggressively toward other dogs later in life. In contrast, if you provide him with positive opportunities to socialize with other puppies during this critical time in his social development, he will have a better understanding of how to interact with other dogs and will be less likely to behave aggressively toward other dogs when he is older.

Situations Where Aggression May Occur

Most dogs do not want to engage in aggression and will try to avoid fighting, but any time two or more dogs meet, aggression may occur. Knowing how your dog reacts in certain situations and what his aggression "hot-spots" are can help you keep your dog under control.

Some dogs react aggressively when they are on a leash, such as when walking with their owners. Other dogs may react aggressively when they are not leashed, such as at an off-leash park. Try to determine whether your dog tends to be more aggressive when he is on or off his leash.

Leash Aggression
• When walking with your dog on a leash, if you and your dog approach another dog that is pulling on his leash, your dog may misinterpret the other dog's straining as aggression and respond aggressively.

Off-Leash Aggression
• When enjoying off-leash playtime, if your dog and another dog try to retrieve the same object, such as a ball or stick, at the same time, the dogs may show aggression toward each other.

• When a new dog tries to join an established group of dogs, fighting may erupt as the dogs attempt to re-establish their status in the new group.

Aggressive Body Language

There are several body language signals you can watch for to determine if your dog is becoming aggressive toward another dog. You will not be able to prevent all dogfights, but with careful observation, you should be able to anticipate aggressive behavior by your dog in time to distract him.

Watch the body language of your dog for the following warning signs of aggression:

• Your dog moves toward another dog slowly and stiffly.

• Your dog's head, ears and tail are raised up.

• Your dog leans forward toward another dog and makes himself seem as large as possible.

• Your dog stares intensely at another dog.

• Your dog growls at another dog.

aggression toward other dogs (continued)

You can help prevent an intense situation between two dogs by responding appropriately when your dog begins to display aggressive behavior. Keeping your physical and emotional responses in check and using commands to control your dog can help keep your dog out of fights before they begin.

Preventing Aggression

If you think your dog may become aggressive, there are several things you can do to help prevent a fight:

• Keep calm. In most situations, your dog will follow your lead. If you are anxious, your dog will sense your anxiety and become more tense.

• Try to keep your breathing normal. People often tend to hold their breath when they sense their dog may fight, which increases your and your dog's stress levels.

• If your dog is on his leash, keep the leash loose. Pulling on the leash may increase your dog's feelings of aggression.

• Do not pet, comfort or otherwise give your dog an extra dose of attention. This common pitfall that dog owners make will likely be interpreted by your dog as a reward, reinforcing the unwanted behavior and encouraging him to repeat it.

Using Commands to Avoid Aggression

Most dogs do not want to engage in aggression and will try to avoid fighting. You can use simple commands to help your dog avoid a fight. If your dog is off his leash, use the Come command (page 116) to call your dog to you. Make sure you reward your dog when he chooses to come to you and avoid aggression. Then attach the leash to your dog's collar and remove him from the situation.

When your dog is on his leash, use the "Let's Go" command, (page 110) and walk away from the other dog. This prevents the dogs from making eye contact. If your dog is already walking with you, get your dog's attention by walking faster or making a turn. Getting your dog's attention will take his attention away from the other dog.

When a Fight Occurs

In general, a noisy fight, with a lot of snarling and growling, is usually less serious than a quiet, intense fight. A noisy fight usually means that the dogs have good bite inhibition and serious injury is less likely to occur. For information on bite inhibition, see page 82. Quiet, intense fights are often more dangerous and may result in more serious injury.

If your dog is engaged in a fight, do not attempt to break up the fight by grabbing your dog's collar or by putting yourself between the dogs. You may get bitten. Instead, try to distract the dogs by making a loud noise, such as shouting or banging garbage can lids together. You can also try splashing water on the dogs using a hose or bucket. When the dogs are apart, you can use the Come command to call your dog to you.

After a Fight

After a fight, give your dog some time and space to calm down. Just after the fight, he probably is not ready to resume normal relations, even with his owner. When he is calm again, examine your dog thoroughly. Take your dog to your veterinarian immediately if you find any potentially serious wounds, such as a puncture wound or a deep bite mark.

Responsible Dog Ownership

As your dog's owner, you are responsible for his behavior, so you should take any act of aggressive behavior by your dog seriously. You cannot make excuses for any incidence of fighting or other aggressive behavior. Try not to worry if your dog gets into a few harmless scuffles with other dogs. However, if your dog starts getting into a lot of seemingly harmless scuffles or participates in a single dangerous fight and inflicts serious injury on the other dog you should seek out the advice of your veterinarian, an animal behaviorist or a qualified dog trainer for help with your dog's behavior.

resource guarding

Resource guarding refers to a dog acting in a possessive and potentially threatening manner when he has an item, such as his food bowl, and someone approaches. A dog may also resource guard a piece of furniture or a specific person. Resource guarding can be a serious behavior problem if left unchecked.

Resource Guarding Food or Toys

To help prevent resource guarding of food or toys, you should feed your dog and allow him to play with toys in an area of your home where people are constantly passing by, such as the kitchen. Giving your dog his food or a toy and then leaving him alone confirms to your dog that the food or toy is his and his only. When your dog is finished eating or playing, put his food bowl or toy away. Leaving food dishes or toys on the floor may encourage resource guarding.

Resource Guarding Furniture

Dogs may also resource guard the furniture where they relax or sleep, such as a bed or couch. If your dog acts possessively of a piece of furniture, you should not allow him up on the furniture until he stops the guarding behavior. To help prevent resource guarding of furniture, you should make your dog earn the privilege of being on the furniture. For example, if your dog wants to get on the couch, ask him to perform a few commands beforehand. You should never give your dog couch time for free.

Resource Guarding People

A dog may also resource guard a person, such as his owner. There is a difference between a protective dog, who is naturally calm and responsive to his owner, and a possessive dog, who acts in a menacing or aggressive manner toward others. If your dog acts in a possessive or threatening manner when another person or dog approaches you, your dog could be resource guarding you. Do not encourage this behavior by coddling or comforting your dog. Remove yourself from your dog so he has nothing to guard.

Early Signs of Resource Guarding

Resource guarding, whether of food, toys, furniture or people, is progressive. This means a dog acts in an increasingly possessive and even threatening manner when he has certain items. If your dog is younger than 18 weeks or displays only the early signs of resource guarding, there are several ways you can prevent resource guarding from becoming a serious problem. For information on preventing resource guarding, see page 228.

Early signs of resource guarding include:

• Eating very fast and even faster when someone approaches.

• Hunching up over food or a toy when someone approaches.

• Stiffening up when someone approaches the item or person the dog is close to.

When Resource Guarding is a Serious Problem

There are several signs that resource guarding has become a serious problem. You should never directly confront a resource guarding dog as he may bite if pushed beyond his comfort level. Resource guarding is especially dangerous if the dog may come into contact with children. Children often do not recognize the signs of resource guarding and are more vulnerable than adults to a dog bite. If your dog's resource guarding is a serious problem, you should seek help from a trained professional, such as a certified animal behaviorist, qualified dog trainer or veterinarian.

Signs that resource guarding has become a serious problem include:

• The dog stiffens and gives a hard stare when someone approaches an item or person he is close to.

• The dog hunches up over his food or toy and growls when someone approaches.

• The dog displays any behavior you find intimidating or threatening when you approach him while he is eating, has a toy, is on furniture or is with a specific person.

resource guarding *(continued)*

Resource guarding is easier to prevent than correct. You should avoid allowing your dog to think that items, such as his food bowl and toys, are his to possess and guard.

Ideally, you want to work with a puppy or a dog that has not already developed the habit of resource guarding. If your dog already shows signs of serious resource guarding, do not perform the steps below—seek the help of a trained professional. For information on the signs of serious resource guarding, see page 227.

You can prevent your dog from guarding his food bowl by teaching him that having people around his food bowl is a pleasurable experience.

For example, approach your dog's food bowl while he is eating, pet him briefly and drop a treat in his bowl. You can also hand feed your dog a portion of each meal or pick up the bowl, mix in a special food and return the bowl to him.

To prevent your dog from guarding toys, practice the Give command. This helps your dog become comfortable giving up his toys and teaches him that toys are not his possessions. For information on the Give command, see page 114.

- If your dog is younger than 18 weeks or displays only the early signs of resource guarding, there are several ways you can prevent your dog from guarding his food.

- Hand feeding your dog a portion of his meal helps your dog become comfortable with human hands in and around his food bowl.

1 Sit on the floor next to your dog and his food bowl.

2 Put your hand in the food bowl and take out some food.

3 Feed your dog from your hand.

- Dropping a treat into your dog's food bowl teaches your dog that good things happen when people approach his food bowl.

1 While your dog is eating, walk up to your dog.

2 Pet your dog briefly and drop a treat into his food.

- To get your dog accustomed to having different people approach his food bowl, various members of your family, starting with the adults, can perform steps 1 and 2.

Tip

What can I do to prevent resource guarding of toys?

To prevent your dog from resource guarding toys, you can play the Trading game (page 137) and Fetch (page 142). Playing the Trading game teaches your dog that it is okay for humans to take his toys since he may get something better in return. Fetch teaches your dog that he does not own his toys. You should play these games with your dog before he develops a guarding habit.

My dog acts possessive of our couch. Is this resource guarding?

Yes. Dogs can also resource guard sleeping areas, which may include crates, beds and couches. If your dog acts possessive of the couch, you should not allow him up on the couch until he stops the guarding behavior. If the behavior does not stop, seek the help of a professional.

To help prevent resource guarding, you should make your dog earn all of the things he considers to be rewards, such as treats, couch time and walks. For example, if your dog wants to get on the couch, he must perform a few commands beforehand. You should never give him any rewards for free.

- Taking your dog's food bowl to add a treat teaches your dog that good things happen when people take his food bowl and that the food bowl is not his possession.

1 While your dog is eating, walk up to your dog.

2 Pick up your dog's food bowl.

3 Place a special food treat in the food bowl.

4 Place the food bowl down so your dog can continue eating.

- Practicing the Give command helps your dog become comfortable giving up toys and teaches your dog that toys are not his possessions.

1 When your dog has a toy in his mouth, hold a treat close to your dog's nose and say the command "Give."

- Your dog drops the toy to take the treat.

2 Give your dog the treat and praise him.

3 Give the toy back to your dog.

living with an aging dog

The way you raise and care for your dog throughout his life can help ensure a smoother transition into his older years. If you have established a regular and healthy routine for your dog's exercise, diet, training and medical care, you can more quickly note changes to that routine as he ages. These changes usually include his eating, sleeping and eliminating patterns, how he plays, how he handles obstacles such as stairs and how well he sees after dark.

In addition to more common signs of aging, such as a graying muzzle and reduced hearing and eyesight, your dog may suffer from some more serious ailments related to aging. These common yet serious complaints include cataracts, muscle atrophy, hormonal imbalances and kidney problems. Dental decay is also a significant problem in older dogs, but is largely preventable by practicing good oral hygiene.

If your dog is diagnosed with a life-threatening illness, be prepared for a serious discussion with your veterinarian about the level of your dog's suffering, the quality of his life and the financial commitment you will make to care for him.

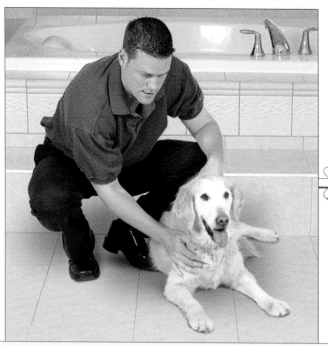

- As your dog ages, you may notice several physical changes. Your dog's muzzle may become gray, his eyes may become cloudy and he may start gaining or losing weight.

- Your dog's energy level may decrease and he may walk stiffly. He may also be sensitive to changes in temperature and have increased toileting needs.

- To help keep your dog healthy, continue with regular veterinary visits and report any problems your dog is experiencing. Also consult your veterinarian about any medications, vaccinations or tests your dog may need.

- Continue with your dog's dental hygiene routine and have your veterinarian regularly check and clean your dog's teeth.

Tip

What else can I do for my aging dog?

Take steps to keep his life as stress-free as possible. For example, if you need to travel for an extended time, consider hiring a house sitter who can watch over your dog. This allows your dog to remain in his home environment rather than going to a kennel or traveling to an unfamiliar location with you. Also, if he is eliminating more frequently and you are away for most of the day, hire a dog walker or ask a neighbor to take your dog outside during the day.

What are some special considerations for dogs losing eyesight or hearing?

Make sure your dog is up to speed with the verbal command and hand signals for basic commands, such as the Sit command and the Come command. These commands will be a comfort to him as his vision and hearing become less reliable. Make his life less stressful by keeping your furniture in the same position as it was before his eyesight started to deteriorate. If your dog is losing his hearing, warn him of your presence by stamping on the floor.

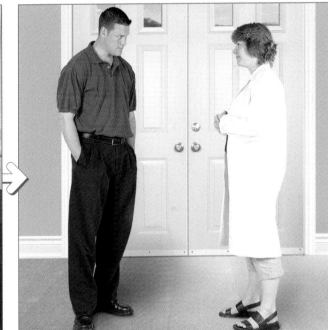

- Continue your handling (page 78) and grooming (page 32) routines so you can quickly identify any changes in your dog.

- Modify your dog's exercise to accommodate his limitations, but keep him reasonably active. Physical activity will improve his circulation, provide mental stimulation and control weight gain.

- Maintain your dog's healthy diet. You may want to consider a dog food specifically made for older dogs.

- If your older dog becomes seriously ill, your veterinarian can be a compassionate source of information and can offer options for you to consider regarding your dog.

- When making difficult decisions about a seriously ill dog, remember to consider his quality of life and the amount of pain and discomfort he may be suffering.

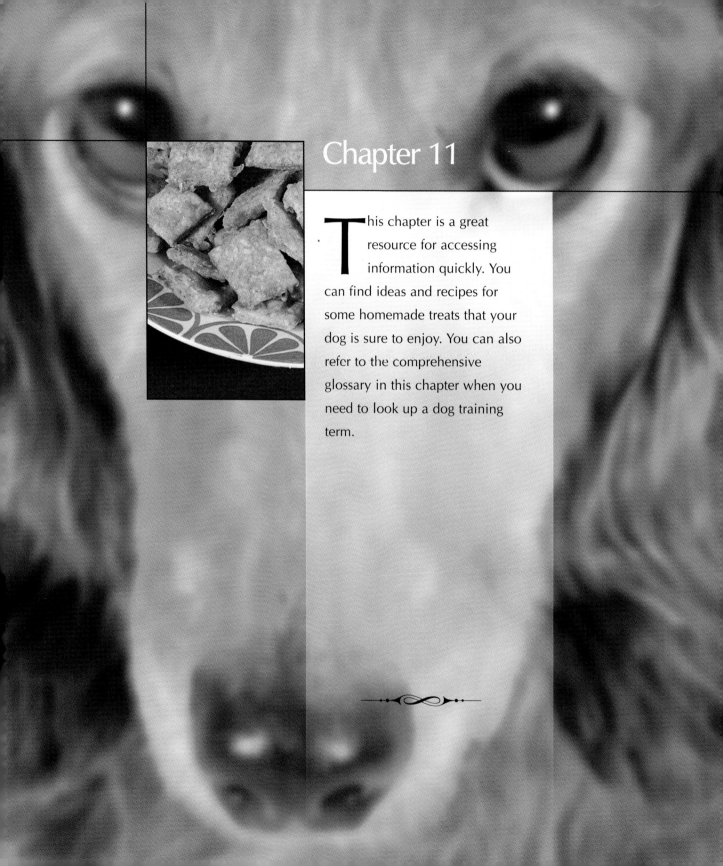

Chapter 11

This chapter is a great resource for accessing information quickly. You can find ideas and recipes for some homemade treats that your dog is sure to enjoy. You can also refer to the comprehensive glossary in this chapter when you need to look up a dog training term.

Recipes and Reference

In this Chapter...

dog treat recipes

Plenty of variations of commercial dog treats are available at your local grocery store or pet supply store. However, making your own treats for your dog can be more rewarding, both for you and your dog. By making your own, you can be confident in the quality of the ingredients in the treats. This allows your dog to have treats made from products that his owners also enjoy, rather than store-bought dog treats that may not be made with human-grade ingredients.

The recipes below introduce a few basic dog treats that you can start with when you want to make your own. You should create a hierarchy of food treats, as all food treats are not created equal. Consider reserving the tasty homemade treats for tricky new behaviors or for special games and tricks.

After you have finished making the wiener, liver and cheesy garlic treats, you can store them in a sealed container in your refrigerator. The treats should last in your refrigerator for up to one week.

Kong™ Stuffing

1 Place a piece of dog biscuit in the bottom of the Kong™ to cover its small hole.

2 Smear the inside of the Kong™ with processed cheese or peanut butter.

3 Add your dog's regular food, plus some surprises, such as apple pieces, hard cheese or carrots.

4 Use dog biscuits to plug the hole in the top of the Kong™.

Wiener Treats

1 Slice half of a package of chicken wieners into 1/2-inch thick coins.

2 Place a piece of paper towel on a microwave-safe plate and place the wiener coins on top of the paper towel.

3 Cover the wiener coins with another piece of paper towel.

4 Microwave at medium-high temperature for five minutes.

5 Cut the cooked coins into quarters.

Tip

What other resources are available for finding homemade dog treat recipes?

There are many dog-friendly recipes available on the Internet. Dog lovers ranging from owners to trainers to dog book publishers are willing to offer a few recipes for your consideration. You will find everything from full meals to cookies and muffins to simple treats such as those described below. There are also many doggie bakeries that offer high quality human grade dog treats.

Can I fancy up some of the treats I make for my dog?

You can easily make your treats a little more visually appealing. For example, if you are making cookies for your dog, you can use cookie cutters to create fancy shapes, rather than simply cutting them into squares. Make sure the shapes you choose do not have sharp edges and angles that could scratch your dog's mouth and throat. You also want to make a cookie or other treat that is sufficiently big enough for your dog. If the treat is too small, your dog may try to swallow it whole.

Liver Treats

Cheesy Garlic Treats

1 Slice 1/2 pound of liver into 1/2-inch wide pieces.

2 Place the liver pieces in a pot of cold water and then bring the water to a boil, stirring often.

3 Turn down the heat and simmer until the liver is cooked thoroughly.

4 Drain the liver and place on a greased baking sheet. Then sprinkle generously with garlic powder.

5 Place the baking sheet in a 300°F oven for 30 minutes.

1 Grate 1 1/2 cups of cheddar cheese.

2 Mix the cheese with 1/2 cup of margarine, one crushed clove of garlic, a pinch of salt and 1 1/2 cups of whole wheat flour.

3 Add enough milk to create a ball of dough.

4 On a floured surface, roll out the dough to 1/4 inch and cut the dough into 1-inch squares.

5 Place the treats on a baking sheet and bake in a 375°F oven for 15 to 20 minutes.

glossary of terms

A

Agility Trial A timed event in which you take your dog through an obstacle course. Your dog is judged based on his speed and how well he keeps on the course.

American Kennel Club The American Kennel Club (AKC) is a not-for-profit organization that maintains the world's largest registry, or list, of purebred dogs. The AKC also administers tests, competitions and other activities for purebred dogs and their owners.

Animal Shelter An organization that cares for puppies and dogs of all types until permanent homes can be found.

Attention Word A word you can use to get your dog to look at you, such as his name.

B

Back Up The command you use to have your dog walk backwards away from you. This is a trick you can teach your dog.

Begging Any unwanted behavior your dog uses to try to obtain food or attention, such as staring, whining or pawing at you.

Bite Inhibition Your dog's ability to control his bite and use his mouth softly. You should begin teaching your dog to control his bite when he is a puppy.

Bite Threshold The level of stress a dog can handle before he bites.

Body Harness A management tool that allows you to control your dog's body to help prevent him from pulling on the leash.

Breed A type of dog. For example, Golden Retriever is one breed of dog and Chihuahua is another.

Breed Rescue Group An organization that cares for abandoned puppies and dogs of a specific breed, or type, until permanent homes can be found.

Breeder A person who raises dogs of a specific breed, or type. Reputable breeders are very concerned about the welfare of their dogs and comply with the established standard for the breed.

Buster® Cube A hollow, cube-shaped toy you can fill with kibble.

C

Canine Good Citizen® A test designed to recognize dogs that have good manners. The test is administered by the American Kennel Club and is made up of a series of 10 tests that the dog must pass to receive the Canine Good Citizen title.

Catch The command you use to have your dog catch an item in his mouth. This is a trick you can teach your dog.

Come The command you use to have your dog stop what he is doing and return to you. A common obedience command.

Competitive Obedience An event that involves you and your dog completing a series of exercises, while being judged on the precision of the performance. There are various levels of competition.

Confinement Area An area of your home with easily cleaned floors, such as a laundry room, where you can keep an unhousetrained dog when you are away from home for an extended period of time.

Conformation An event your purebred dog can participate in. Dogs are judged on how well they meet their breed standard, which is a written description of the ideal dog, including qualities such as body length, coat color and temperament.

Cookie on Paw A trick you can teach your dog that allows him to practice self control and the Off command.

Crate A plastic, fiberglass or metal box that has a door you can close to keep your dog inside. A crate is useful for housetraining and for preventing inappropriate behavior when you cannot supervise your dog.

Crate Training Teaching your dog to be comfortable in his crate so he will eventually automatically go to his crate to relax or sleep.

Crawl The command you use to have your dog pull himself along the floor. This is a trick you can teach your dog.

D **Dance** The command you use to have your dog stand up on his hind legs. This is a trick you can teach your dog.

Digging Pit A designated area of your yard where your dog is allowed to dig. Providing a digging pit is useful if your dog is prone to destructive digging in other areas of your yard.

Distractions When training, you can introduce visual distractions, such as squatting down in front of your dog, and sound distractions, such as clapping, to ensure your dog will respond to your commands even when faced with real-life diversions.

Do Your Business The command you use to have your dog eliminate on cue. A housetraining command.

Down The command you use to have your dog lie on the ground, with his abdomen touching the ground and his hind legs tucked under his body. A basic obedience command.

Drafting An event in which dogs pull an item, such as a cart, through a course. During a competition, dogs must cooperate while being hitched up to equipment and be able to back up and change speeds while pulling the equipment.

E **Earthdog Trial** An event for dogs originally bred to hunt small animals hiding in tunnels or dens, such as rats. Dogs are judged on their ability to track and locate small animals.

Exercise Pen A foldable fence you can set up indoors or outdoors to give your dog a confined area that he can move around in.

F **Fetch** A game you can play with your dog that allows your dog to practice returning to you and giving you an item.

Field Trial An event that allows hunting dogs to demonstrate their skills of tracking and retrieving game birds.

Flyball A relay race in which teams consisting of four dogs compete against each other. Each dog races over a set of hurdles, steps on a board to launch a ball into the air and then returns to the starting position.

Flying Disc A competition in which you throw Frisbees® for your dog to catch. Flying Disc competitions can consist of timed catch and retrieve events and choreographed freestyle events.

Front and Center A game you can play with your dog that allows your dog to practice walking on a loose leash, paying attention to you and coming when called.

glossary of terms

G

Give The command you use to have your dog drop an item that is in his mouth. A common obedience command.

Go To Your Place The command you use to send your dog to a specific location, such as a mat, where he should remain until he is released. A more advanced obedience command.

Grooming Keeping your dog clean by performing tasks such as brushing his coat, trimming his nails, caring for his teeth and bathing him.

H

Handling Teaching your dog to be comfortable with being touched by you or someone else.

Head Halter A management tool that allows you to control your dog's head to help prevent him from pulling on the leash.

Heel The command you use to have your dog walk close to your left side, with his ear lined up with the side seam of your pants and his attention focused on you. A more advanced obedience command.

Herding Trial An event in which herding dogs can demonstrate their ability to move livestock through a series of gates and into a confinement area.

Here The command you use to have your dog come directly and instantly to you. An emergency obedience command.

Hide and Seek A game you can play with your dog that allows your dog to practice coming when called and keeping track of your location.

High Five The command you use to have your dog raise his front paw to connect with your palm. This is a trick you can teach your dog.

Housetraining Teaching your dog to eliminate in his outdoor toilet area.

How Do You Do A game you can play with your dog that allows your dog to practice sitting politely in front of people, instead of jumping up on them.

Hugs The command you use to have your dog jump up and place his front paws on you. This is a trick you can teach your dog.

K

Kong™ A hollow, rubber chew toy you can fill with treats or kibble.

Kong™ Hunt A mentally stimulating activity for your dog in which you hide a chew toy filled with treats for your dog to find.

L

Let's Go The command you use to have your dog walk politely with you, without your dog pulling on the leash. A common obedience command.

Life Reward An activity your dog enjoys, such as chewing a toy, going for a walk or playing a game. You can give your dog a life reward, instead of food, when he responds to a command or displays appropriate behavior. *See also* Reward.

Limited-Slip Collar This type of collar safely tightens around a dog's neck when the dog pulls back on his leash. Also called a martingale or greyhound collar.

Long Line A 15 to 30 foot line you can attach to your dog's collar. When training, a long line allows you to move away from your dog while still maintaining control. Use a long line only when you can supervise your dog.

Lure When you first start training your dog to perform a command, you will usually use a lure to guide him into position. Using a lure allows you to show your dog what to do without using your hands or a leash to push or pull him into position. You will often use a food treat as a lure.

Lure Coursing A competition in which sighthounds, such as Greyhounds, chase a lure around an outdoor course while being judged on their enthusiasm, speed and endurance.

M

Mixed Breed Dog A dog whose parents are different breeds, or types, of dog. For example, a Cockapoo has a Cocker Spaniel parent and a Poodle parent.

Mouthing Play biting and nipping by puppies. Mouthing is a natural, normal puppy behavior.

Move The command you use to have your dog step aside when he is in your way. A common obedience command.

Musical Freestyle An event in which you and your dog perform a choreographed routine to music that highlights your dog's obedience skills and abilities.

O

Off The command you use to have your dog back away from an item you do not want him to touch. A common obedience command.

Off-Leash Park A designated area where you can allow your dog to play and socialize off his leash. Also called a dog run or dog park.

Off-Leash Training Training commands, such as Sit, Stand, Down, Stay and Come, in a safe area outdoors with your dog off his leash.

Outside The command you use to stop your dog when he is eliminating in an inappropriate area, such as in the house, so you can take him outdoors. A housetraining command.

Over The command you use to have your dog jump over an obstacle. This is a trick you can teach your dog.

P

Paper Training Teaching your dog to eliminate on newspaper, cat litter or another absorbent material when using an outdoor toilet area is not practical.

Play Possum The command you use to have your dog lie down on his side, with his head resting on the floor. This is a trick you can teach your dog.

Positive Training Rewarding your dog with food, toys or an enjoyable activity when he responds to a command or acts in an appropriate manner to reinforce his good behavior. Also, using positive responses, such as removing your dog from a situation, when he acts inappropriately.

Puppy Push-Ups A game you can play with your dog that allows your dog to practice the Sit command and the Down command.

Purebred Dog A dog whose mother, father and ancestors are all the same breed, or type, of dog.

R

Rally Obedience A relaxed form of obedience competition that emphasizes teamwork between the dog and his owner. Also called Rally-O.

Read A fun, basic trick you can teach your dog in which your dog seems to be reading.

Recall Game A game you can play with your dog that allows your dog to practice the Come command.

Release Word A word you can use at the end of a stationary command, such as Stay, to tell your dog he is now free to move.

Resource Guarding A dog's unwanted behavior of acting in a possessive and eventually threatening manner when he has an item, such as his food bowl, and someone approaches. Dogs may also resource guard people and furniture. Resource guarding can be a serious behavior problem that requires professional help to overcome.

Reward A reward can be praise or an item your dog likes, such as food or a toy. When training, you give your dog a reward when he responds to a command so he will be more likely to respond to the command in the future. *See also* Life Reward.

Roll Over The command you use to have your dog turn from one side onto his other side while he is lying on the ground. This is a trick you can teach your dog.

Schutzhund Trial A specialized competition for dog breeds commonly used in police work, such as German Shepherds. Dogs compete in tracking, obedience and protection activities.

Search and Rescue Challenging public service work that requires a dog to enter potentially dangerous situations with his owner in order to save people who are injured or lost.

Separation Anxiety A dog's feelings of stress and panic when he is left alone. Excessive panting, pacing, barking and destructive behavior can be signs of separation anxiety. Separation anxiety can be a serious behavior problem that requires professional help to overcome.

Settle The command you use to have your dog calm down when he is excited and lie on the ground in a comfortable position. A common obedience command.

Shake a Paw The command you use to have your dog raise his front paw into the air so you can catch and shake his paw. This is a trick you can teach your dog.

Shaping Teaching your dog a command by breaking the command into small steps to help ensure your dog's success.

Shell Game A mentally stimulating activity for your dog in which you hide a biscuit under one of three plastic containers and allow your dog to determine which container the biscuit is under.

Shush The command you use to have your dog stop barking. An obedience command.

Sit The command you use to have your dog sit with his hind quarters on the ground. The most basic obedience command.

Sit Pretty The command you use to have your dog raise his front paws off the floor and balance on his hind quarters. This is a trick you can teach your dog.

Skijoring An event in which a person wearing cross-country skis is harnessed to one or more dogs that pull the person through a course. The team with the best time through the course wins the competition.

Sled Dog Racing A competition in which a team of dogs pulls a sled and driver.

S

Socialization Teaching your dog to be comfortable with a variety of places, situations, people and sounds. Socialization is the key to having a stable, reliable dog and should be the top priority in your early training process.

Speak The command you use to have your dog bark on cue. This is a trick you can teach your dog.

Spin The command you use to have your dog walk in a counter-clockwise circle. This is a trick you can teach your dog.

Stand The command you use to have your dog stand. A basic obedience command.

Stay The command you use to have your dog remain in a position, such as the Sit, Down or Stand position, until you release him. A common obedience command.

T

Take a Bow The command you use to have your dog lower his chest to the floor, while keeping his hind quarters in the air, as if he were taking a bow. This is a trick you can teach your dog.

Take It The command you use to have your dog use his mouth to take an item, such as food or a toy, from your hand.

Therapy Dog A dog who brings comfort and companionship to people who are confined to hospitals or nursing homes. Also called Visiting dogs.

Touch The command you use to have your dog touch a target, such as your hand, with his nose. A more advanced obedience command.

Tracking A dog's ability to follow scents for hunters or in competition. Also refers to a mentally stimulating activity for your dog in which you leave a trail of food for your dog to follow.

Tracking Trial An event in which dogs compete to see who can successfully follow a scent. Dogs of all types who enjoy following a scent can participate in many tracking events.

Trading Game A game you can play with your dog that allows your dog to practice giving you an item in exchange for another item.

Tug A game you can play with your dog that allows your dog to practice self control and giving up an item.

Turn The command you use to have your dog walk in a clockwise circle. This is a trick you can teach your dog.

W

Wait The command you use to have your dog stay where he is until you give another command. A more advanced obedience command.

Wave The command you use to have your dog move his paw up and down in the air in a waving motion. This is a trick you can teach your dog.

Weave The command you use to have your dog walk between your legs, alternating between the right and left leg in a figure-eight formation.

index

index

index

index

Did you like this book? MARAN ILLUSTRATED™ offers books on the most popular computer topics, using the same easy-to-use format of this book. We always say that if you like one of our books, you'll love the rest of our books too!

Here's a list of some of our best-selling computer titles:

Guided Tour Series - 240 pages, Full Color

MARAN ILLUSTRATED's Guided Tour series features a friendly disk character that walks you through each task step by step. The full-color screen shots are larger than in any of our other series and are accompanied by clear, concise instructions.

	ISBN-10	ISBN-13	Price
MARAN ILLUSTRATED™ Computers Guided Tour	1-59200-880-1	978-1-59200-880-3	$24.99 US/$33.95 CDN
MARAN ILLUSTRATED™ Windows XP Guided Tour	1-59200-886-0	978-1-59200-886-5	$24.99 US/$33.95 CDN

MARAN ILLUSTRATED™ Series - 320 pages, Full Color

This series covers 30% more content than our Guided Tour series. Learn new software fast using our step-by-step approach and easy-to-understand text. Learning programs has never been this easy!

	ISBN-10	ISBN-13	Price
MARAN ILLUSTRATED™ Access 2003	1-59200-872-0	978-1-59200-872-8	$24.99 US/$33.95 CDN
MARAN ILLUSTRATED™ Computers	1-59200-874-7	978-1-59200-874-2	$24.99 US/$33.95 CDN
MARAN ILLUSTRATED™ Excel 2003	1-59200-876-3	978-1-59200-876-6	$24.99 US/$33.95 CDN
MARAN ILLUSTRATED™ Mac OS® X v.10.4 Tiger™	1-59200-878-X	978-1-59200-878-0	$24.99 US/$33.95 CDN
MARAN ILLUSTRATED™ Office 2003	1-59200-890-9	978-1-59200-890-2	$29.99 US/$39.95 CDN
MARAN ILLUSTRATED™ Windows XP	1-59200-870-4	978-1-59200-870-4	$24.99 US/$33.95 CDN

101 Hot Tips Series - 240 pages, Full Color

Progress beyond the basics with MARAN ILLUSTRATED's 101 Hot Tips series. This series features 101 of the coolest shortcuts, tricks and tips that will help you work faster and easier.

	ISBN-10	ISBN-13	Price
MARAN ILLUSTRATED™ Windows XP 101 Hot Tips	1-59200-882-8	978-1-59200-882-7	$19.99 US/$26.95 CDN

MARAN ILLUSTRATED™ **Piano**
is an information-packed resource
for people who want to learn to
play the piano, as well as current
musicians looking to hone their skills.
Combining full-color photographs and
easy-to-follow instructions, this guide
covers everything from the basics
of piano playing to more advanced
techniques. Not only does MARAN
ILLUSTRATED™ Piano show you how
to read music, play scales and chords
and improvise while playing with
other musicians, it also provides
you with helpful information for
purchasing and caring for your piano.

ISBN-10: 1-59200-864-X
ISBN-13: 978-1-59200-864-3
Price: $24.99 US; $33.95 CDN
Page count: 304

MARAN ILLUSTRATED™ **Dog Training**
is an excellent guide for both current
dog owners and people considering
making a dog part of their family.
Using clear, step-by-step instructions
accompanied by over 400 full-color
photographs, MARAN ILLUSTRATED™
Dog Training is perfect for any visual
learner who prefers seeing what to do
rather than reading lengthy explanations.

Beginning with insights into popular
dog breeds and puppy development,
this book emphasizes positive training
methods to guide you through
socializing, housetraining and teaching
your dog many commands. You will
also learn how to work with problem
behaviors, such as destructive chewing.

ISBN-10: 1-59200-858-5
ISBN-13: 978-1-59200-858-2
Price: $19.99 US; $26.95 CDN
Page count: 256

MARAN ILLUSTRATED™ Knitting & Crocheting contains a wealth of information about these two increasingly popular crafts. Whether you are just starting out or you are an experienced knitter or crocheter interested in picking up new tips and techniques, this information-packed resource will take you from the basics, such as how to hold the knitting needles or crochet hook, to more advanced skills, such as how to add decorative touches to your projects. The easy-to-follow information is communicated through clear, step-by-step instructions and accompanied by over 600 full-color photographs—perfect for any visual learner.

ISBN-10: 1-59200-862-3

ISBN-13: 978-1-59200-862-9

Price: $24.99 US; $33.95 CDN

Page count: 304

MARAN ILLUSTRATED™ Yoga provides a wealth of simplified, easy-to-follow information about the increasingly popular practice of Yoga. This easy-to-use guide is a must for visual learners who prefer to see and do without having to read lengthy explanations.

Using clear, step-by-step instructions accompanied by over 500 full-color photographs, this book includes all the information you need to get started with yoga or to enhance your technique if you have already made yoga a part of your life. MARAN ILLUSTRATED™ Yoga shows you how to safely and effectively perform a variety of yoga poses at various skill levels, how to breathe more efficiently and much more.

ISBN-10: 1-59200-868-2

ISBN-13: 978-1-59200-868-1

Price: $24.99 US; $33.95 CDN

Page count: 320

MARAN ILLUSTRATED™ Weight Training is an information-packed guide that covers all the basics of weight training, as well as more advanced techniques and exercises.

MARAN ILLUSTRATED™ Weight Training contains more than 500 full-color photographs of exercises for every major muscle group, along with clear, step-by-step instructions for performing the exercises. Useful tips provide additional information and advice to help enhance your weight training experience.

MARAN ILLUSTRATED™ Weight Training provides all the information you need to start weight training or to refresh your technique if you have been weight training for some time.

ISBN-10: 1-59200-866-6
ISBN-13: 978-1-59200-866-7
Price: $24.99 US; $33.95 CDN
Page count: 320

MARAN ILLUSTRATED™ Poker is an essential resource that covers all aspects of the most popular poker games, including Texas Hold'em, Omaha and Seven-Card Stud. You will also find valuable information on playing in tournaments, bluffing, feeling at home in a casino and even playing poker online.

This information-packed guide includes hundreds of detailed, full-color illustrations accompanying the step-by-step instructions that walk you through each topic. MARAN ILLUSTRATED™ Poker is a must-have for anyone who prefers a visual approach to learning rather than simply reading explanations.

Whether you are a novice getting ready to join in a friend's home game or you are an experienced poker player looking to hone your tournament skills, MARAN ILLUSTRATED™ Poker provides all the poker information you need.

ISBN-10: 1-59200-946-8
ISBN-13: 978-1-59200-946-6
Price: $19.99 US; $26.95 CD
Page count: 240

MARAN ILLUSTRATED™ Guitar is an excellent resource for people who want to learn to play the guitar, as well as for current musicians who want to fine tune their technique. This full-color guide includes over 500 photographs, accompanied by step-by-step instructions that teach you the basics of playing the guitar and reading music, as well as advanced guitar techniques. You will also learn what to look for when purchasing a guitar or accessories, how to maintain and repair your guitar, and much more.

Whether you want to learn to strum your favorite tunes or play professionally, MARAN ILLUSTRATED™ Guitar provides all the information you need to become a proficient guitarist.

ISBN-10: 1-59200-860-7

ISBN-13: 978-1-59200-860-5

Price: $24.99 US; $33.95 CDN

Page count: 320

MARAN ILLUSTRATED™ Cooking Basics is an information-packed resource that covers all the basics of cooking. Novices and experienced cooks alike will find useful information about setting up and stocking your kitchen as well as food preparation and cooking techniques. With over 500 full-color photographs illustrating the easy-to-follow, step-by-step instructions, this book is a must-have for anyone who prefers seeing what to do rather than reading long explanations.

MARAN ILLUSTRATED™ Cooking Basics also provides over 40 recipes from starters, salads and side-dishes to main course dishes and baked goods. Each recipe uses only 10 ingredients or less, and is complete with nutritional information and tips covering tasty variations and commonly asked questions.

ISBN-10: 1-59863-234-5

ISBN-13: 978-1-59863-234-7

Price: $19.99 US; $26.95 CDN

Page count: 240

MARAN ILLUSTRATED™ Effortless Algebra is an indispensable resource packed with crucial concepts and step-by-step instructions that make learning algebra simple. This easy-to-use guide is perfect for those who wish to gain a thorough understanding of algebra's concepts, from the most basic calculations to more complex operations.

Clear instructions thoroughly explain every topic and each concept is accompanied by helpful illustrations. This book provides all of the information you will need to fully grasp algebra, whether you are new to the subject or have been solving quadratic equations for years. MARAN ILLUSTRATED™ Effortless Algebra also provides an abundance of practice examples and tests so that you can put your knowledge into practice. This book is a must-have resource for any student of algebra.

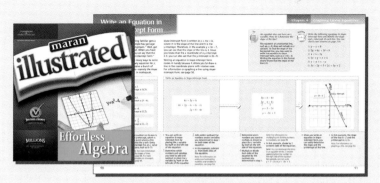

ISBN-10: 1-59200-942-5
ISBN-13: 978-1-59200-942-8
Price: $24.99 US; $33.95 CDN
Page count: 304

MARAN ILLUSTRATED™ Sudoku is an excellent resource for anyone who wants to learn how to solve Sudoku puzzles or improve their skills.

This book contains easy-to-follow instructions explaining how to play Sudoku as well as advanced puzzle-solving strategies. The colorful illustrations and step-by-step instructions are perfect for any visual learner. MARAN ILLUSTRATED™ Sudoku also contains over 100 puzzles and answers so you can put your new Sudoku skills to the test!

Whether you have never tried a Sudoku puzzle before or you are an experienced player, MARAN ILLUSTRATED™ Sudoku is the book for you.

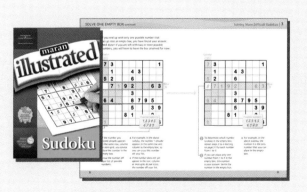

ISBN-10: 1-59863-316-3
ISBN-13: 978-1-59863-316-0
Price: $9.99 US; $13.95 CDN
Page count: 192

MARAN ILLUSTRATED™ Bartending
is the perfect book for those who want to
impress their guests with cocktails that are
both eye-catching and delicious. This
indispensable guide explains everything
you need to know about bartending in
the most simple and easy-to-follow terms.
MARAN ILLUSTRATED™ Bartending has
recipes, step-by-step instructions and over
400 full-color photographs of all the hottest
martinis, shooters, blended drinks and
warmers. This guide also includes a
section on wine, beer and alcohol-free
cocktails as well as information on all
of the tools, liquor and other supplies
you will need to start creating drinks
right away!

ISBN-10: 1-59200-944-1
ISBN-13: 978-1-59200-944-2
Price: $19.99 US; $26.95 CDN
Page count: 256